ABOUT
THE AUTHOR

RGH

WALTER RUSSELL BOWIE has written *THE STORY OF THE CHURCH* in response to many requests from people who have used and loved his modern classic, *The Story of the Bible*. They will find in *THE STORY OF THE CHURCH* the same fine scholarship and delightful narrative style that have made the previous book so popular.

Dr. Bowie's wide experience has given him unusual qualifications for writing an accurate, interesting history of the Church for Christians of all ages and all faiths. A graduate of Harvard University and the Theological Seminary of Virginia, he served as rector of Episcopal churches in Greenwood and Richmond, Virginia, and of Grace Church in New York City. From 1939 to 1950 he was professor of practical theology at Union Theological Seminary in New York, where he also served as dean of students for five years. More recently he has been professor of homiletics at the Protestant Episcopal Theological Seminary in Virginia.

Dr. Bowie has had many years of experience in interpreting the wonderful stories of the Bible and the Church to students, to members of his congregations, and to young people, including his own children and grandchildren.

His books, in addition to *The Story of the Bible,* include two Bible story books for younger children, *The Bible Story for Boys and Girls—New Testament* and *The Bible Story for Boys and Girls—Old Testament,* and *Preaching,* a definitive study in homiletics. He is an associate editor of *The Interpreter's Bible* and contributes to many leading magazines.

THE STORY OF THE CHURCH

WALTER RUSSELL BOWIE

ILLUSTRATED BY CLIFFORD JOHNSTON

ABINGDON PRESS
NEW YORK • NASHVILLE

THE STORY OF THE CHURCH

Copyright MCMLV by Pierce & Washabaugh

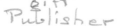

Gift
Publisher

Library of Congress Catalog Card Number: 55-9137

1-16-56

77542

JAN 2 4 '56

BR
150
B78

SET UP, PRINTED, AND BOUND BY THE
PARTHENON PRESS, AT NASHVILLE,
TENNESSEE, UNITED STATES OF AMERICA

TO JEANIE

PREFACE

CROSS THE countryside and in the towns and cities there are many churches. They have various names. Some particular church is the one we know best. We go there to worship, and we love it especially. If we went to another church, it might seem in some ways different and unfamiliar. The looks of the building, what the minister wears, the prayers and the hymns, might seem not quite like those we are used to. But one thing would be the same. We should hear again and again the name of Jesus. We should begin to remember that not only our church but other churches we had not thought about belong to him.

We hear someone say—or we say ourselves—"I belong to a Baptist church." Or to a Congregational church. Or to a Disciples church. Or, "I am an Episcopalian." Or a Methodist. Or a Presbyterian. Or a Roman Catholic. Or some other in the long alphabet of names. But none of these is the greatest name. The church we know best is like a beautiful tree to which we look up and under which we take shelter. But the tree is only part of the forest, and the forest is the fellowship of all those whose life grows out of the love of Jesus Christ.

A forest does what no single tree can do. From its slopes it sends out its influence far beyond its borders. When the snows and the rains come down from the sky, they seep into the rich soil that forms around the roots of all the trees in the deep wood. Those waters feed the brooks and the springs that keep the valleys green in far-off lands where men might forget the forest because it is beyond their sight. But the wells by their front doors have been filled from it; and if the forest were not there, the life of the land would dry up and die.

So it is with the great Church to which all Christian people belong. For more than nineteen hundred years it has been sending the streams of its influence out into the world. It is bigger than any particular part of it. We must take a long look and a wide view to realize the wonder of it. Like trees in a forest, different congregations have grown up in it; but whenever they have been great and good, it has been because their roots went down into the same ground. That ground is the remembrance of Jesus Christ. From him, and from the love of him, through the long centuries the men and women who have been most brave and true have drawn their strength. So this story of the Church starts not with us but with the disciples who first knew Jesus, and he is the meaning of the story from then till now.

WALTER RUSSELL BOWIE

CONTENTS

1. When the World Was Dark 11

2. The Day of Resurrection 17

3. The Spirit Stirs the Disciples 20

4. The Beginning of Persecution . . . 24

5. The Conversion of Saul of Tarsus . . 27

6. A Great Adventurer for Christ . . . 31

7. Journey's End 35

8. Fire and Fury 40

9. Christians Who Dared Death Unafraid 43

10. An Emperor Becomes a Christian . . 48

11. Ambrose and Augustine 55

12. When Men Despaired of Their
    World 60

13. Missionaries of the Gospel 66

14. More Danger for the Christian
    Church 73

15. The Dark Ages 78

16. New Kingdoms Rise in Europe . . . 83

17. Chivalry and the Crusades 88

18. Popes and Emperors 95

19. A Saint Who Made Men Remember
Christ 102

20. Religion in the Middle Ages 109

21. Men Who Dared to Think 113

22. Times of Change 119

23. A New Discoverer of the Gospel . . . 124

24. One Lonely Monk Among the
Mighty 130

25. Other Champions of the New Faith . . 137

26. Conflicts in England and in Scotland . 143

27. The New Army of the Popes 153

28. Puritans and Kings 157

29. The Gospel Comes to the Common
People 168

30. When the Church Saw the Whole
World's Need 176

31. The Meaning of Missions
Rediscovered 182

32. Christian Churches in the United
States 187

33. What the Churches May Be Learning
Now 194

Index 203

CHAPTER 1

WHEN THE WORLD WAS DARK

HE CHURCH began long before there was such a thing as a special building or any other particular place where those who would call themselves members of the Church might be accustomed to come together. It began when Jesus had left the little town of Nazareth to tell people in all the land of Galilee about God, and when he said to some men by the lake of Galilee, "Come, follow me." They did go with him, those first men he called: Peter and Andrew, James and John. They were in their fishing boats that day, and they left their boats and their nets behind. If anyone had asked them, "Where are you going, and why are you going?" they could not have given a very thorough answer. Just one thing they were sure of. When Jesus looked at them and spoke to them, they wanted to be in his company wherever he might go.

One by one more were added—Matthew, Thomas, and the others who with the first four disciples became the Twelve. They were the group that was closest to Jesus. Other men and women also followed him, called by his words and by the answer of their own hearts. Not in name yet but in fact the Church had begun with them.

As they went with Jesus, they heard him teach the people, sometimes in the synagogues, sometimes out in the open places where the crowds flocked about him. They watched him heal the sick and stop to talk to sinners whom respectable folk despised. They saw that the ordinary people listened to him and loved him. But they saw also that some of the proud and powerful began to be offended at him. These were annoyed because Jesus seemed to be saying that people in other nations might be as much the children of God as they themselves were. He praised a Roman centurion and answered an appeal from a Syrophoenician woman. He would break through old customs and stiff ideas

11

if those stood in the way of showing the love of God to any who were in distress. And on the other hand, he spoke the truth of God with terrible plainness to those who pretended to be pious, who said long prayers in the name of God, but all the while were hard and cruel.

As the disciples went with Jesus, he seemed to them every day more great and wonderful. Then one day he asked them what the people were saying about him. They told him that some said he was a new prophet, and some said he must be Elijah or some other mighty man of God come back from the dead.

"But what do you say?" he asked.

Then it was as though a great light broke in Peter's mind. Jesus must be the Messiah—the Deliverer and Savior whom the prophets of Israel had foretold.

"You are the Christ!" he exclaimed.

Now surely—the disciples thought—amazing things would happen. Jesus would rule the earth in a glorious kingdom of the power of God.

But to their dismay Jesus began to tell them something completely different. Because of the sins of men he would have to face hatred and the risk of death. He must be ready to suffer before he could save. In Galilee he might be safe, but he must carry the message of God up to the capital city. There in Jerusalem were men who would destroy him if they could. But he set his face to go to Jerusalem. And the disciples followed him, though they were afraid.

It was the week of Passover, when thousands and thousands of the people of Israel came to Jerusalem from far and near to worship and to thank God for the first Passover when Moses had led their fathers out of Egypt and set them free.

On the road leading into Jerusalem the crowds recognized Jesus. Some of them began to shout around him and to throw down green branches and even their own cloaks to make a triumphal way before him. "Blessed is he who comes in the name of the Lord!" they cried.

The rulers in Jerusalem heard the distant shouting. "What is that?" they wanted to know. When they were told that it was

Jesus of Nazareth who was being welcomed by the people, they were annoyed and sullen. And soon after that their sullenness turned into hot anger. They learned that Jesus had gone to the Temple—the glorious Temple for the worship of God that stood on its hilltop with its marble walls and its golden roof lifted grandly against the sky. There in the Temple he had found its courts filled with loud-voiced traders, selling animals for sacrifice. He said they had made his Father's house a place for haggling and for money-making greed. And he drove the traders and their animals out.

He stood there and taught the people that thronged around him. But the rulers, who had the right to control what went on in the Temple, were furious. Jesus of Nazareth would not teach much longer if they could help it.

The final sacred day of the Passover celebration came. All day long the city had been filled with people. But now it was evening, and the crowds were gone from the streets. Everywhere in the houses lamps were lighted. In families or in little groups of friends people were gathering to eat the Passover supper together.

To a room in a house upstairs came Jesus and his disciples. Usually the Passover supper meant thanksgiving and joyfulness, but now the disciples were not joyful. Not even though Jesus was there. They loved him more than they loved anyone or anything else on earth; and as long as they had him, nothing else could matter. But in their hearts was the heavy fear that soon they might not have him. Something too terrible to think of might be about to happen.

They felt this all the more when Jesus said that he would not eat the Passover supper with them again until they should eat it in the kingdom of heaven. What could that mean except—they could not bear to say it—except that he would die and they would be left alone?

Then—more shocking still—they heard Jesus say, "One of you will betray me." Betray him! Who could possibly do that? They looked at one another as men stunned into silence. Then they saw Judas, one of the Twelve, leave his place at the table

and slip out of the room. They did not know that his loyalty to Jesus had turned sour and that already he had made a bargain with the enemies of his Master.

The lamps burned low, and the shadows were on their troubled faces. Then Jesus rose and led them out. It was dark now in the streets, and dark in the place to which he led them, under old olive trees beyond the city walls, in what was called the garden of Gethsemane. Jesus knelt down to pray. But while he still was praying, what they had been afraid of began to happen, and to happen fast.

There was a noise outside the garden, and a flaring of torches. Armed servants of Caiaphas, the high priest, led by Judas, came through the trees. They took Jesus and led him away to Caiaphas' house, while the disciples scattered, and only Peter followed, but he hoping all the while that he would not be seen. When a servant girl recognized Peter and said that he was one of Jesus' disciples, Peter was panic-stricken and swore that he had nothing to do with Jesus, and then a moment later rushed out and cried as though his heart would break.

It was still night. In the morning the high priest and others with him who wanted to be rid of Jesus took Jesus to the court of Pontius Pilate, the governor who had been appointed by the Roman emperor to have authority in Jerusalem. They brought false charges against Jesus. Pilate believed that they were false, and he saw no reason why Jesus should be condemned. He tried to question him and to find out what his accusers were talking about when they claimed that Jesus had said he was bringing in a new kingdom. The only sort of kingdom Pilate understood was the rule of Rome that depended upon its soldiers' swords and spears. He could not figure out what Jesus meant when he answered, "My kingdom is not of this world," and, "My kingdom is of the truth." All Pilate could do was to shrug his shoulders and make another start.

He brought Jesus out on the balcony of his palace, above the open court where the crowd of his accusers were. On Jesus' head was a crown platted out of thorns that jeering Roman soldiers had been allowed to put there, and his back was bleeding from their whips. Pilate thought that Jesus' enemies would be satisfied. But he did not know how merciless the high priest could be, nor how great was the hatred of the traders who had been driven out of the Temple. When they caught sight of Jesus, they shouted, "Crucify him! Crucify him!"

Pilate was afraid of stirring up more trouble than he could deal with. Nothing was left, he thought, but to let the crowd there in front of him have its way. He sent for a basin of water and washed his hands, as if to say that he was not to blame. He handed Jesus over to the soldiers to be taken to a hill outside the city walls called Calvary. There they nailed him on a cross to die.

Two robbers were crucified on that same hill beside him. The Gospels tell that one of them, as he looked at Jesus, had such a feeling of his greatness that he called out, "Lord, remember me when you come into your kingdom!" and that the Roman centurion in charge of the soldiers said, "Truly this man was a son of God!" But most of those who stood round the cross mocked at Jesus. They shouted to him that if he knew how to come down from his cross, let him do it. They said that he had claimed to save others and now he could not even save himself.

CHAPTER 2

THE DAY OF RESURRECTION

T WAS the morning of the first day of the week, the day that we call Sunday.

Two days before, when Jesus had been crucified, his body had been taken down from the cross and laid in a tomb in a garden outside Jerusalem. Now when it was scarcely dawn on this third day, three of the women who were followers of Jesus went out toward the tomb, carrying sweet spices to put beside his body.

Somewhere in the city, still shocked at Jesus' death and hopeless, the disciples were hiding. If those who had brought Jesus to his cross should find them, they might be put to death too. Anyhow without him there did not seem to be much to live for any more.

Another night was over, and another dawn had come. The sun was climbing over the horizon, and the first long shafts of level light pierced the cold shadows in the city streets. But night or day, what did it matter now that Jesus was gone?

Then outside the house where the disciples were, there was the sound of running feet. Hands were knocking at the door— a quick and eager knocking, yet hushed and guarded lest people near should wake and want to know what this was all about.

"Peter!" came the voices from outside the door. "Peter, John, and all the others, quick! Let us in!"

So the door was opened, and into the room where the disciples were came Mary Magdalene and Salome and another Mary—the three who had gone out that morning to the garden tomb.

"We took our spices to lay beside his body," they said. "We went to anoint the dead, and he is not dead. The tomb was open. His body is not there. Jesus is alive!"

The disciples looked at the women like men who had been

17

stunned. Then they drew in their breath as with a great sob of wonder and amazement. Their faces brightened, as when the sun breaks through the clouds.

"I will go and see," said Peter.

"And I am going with you!" cried John.

So the two of them ran together toward the garden where Jesus' body had been laid. John was the younger, and he outran Peter and came first to the tomb. But he did not dare go in. Then came Peter and burst past him—past him into the shadows of the tomb that was hollowed in the hill. As the women had said, it was empty. The body they had buried was not there.

Peter and John hurried back to the other disciples. There was time now to hear more of what the women had to tell. They said they had seen outside the tomb a figure in a long white robe, like an angel, who told them that the Lord was risen. And Mary Magdalene, going back again, half blinded by her tears, had seen someone she supposed to be the gardener. When she had spoken to him, he had called her name. And looking up at the sound of that voice, she saw that it was not the gardener. It was Jesus!

But the wonder of that day—that first Easter day—was not finished. In the evening two of those who had listened to Jesus and had loved him, but were not among the disciples who had been most closely with him, were on the road away from Jerusalem to the village of Emmaus, where they lived. They had heard of what the women had told about the empty tomb, but how could they quite believe it? For Jesus to be crucified had seemed so awful that it was hard to think of anything but that. Then as they walked on the road while the night was falling, someone whom they did not recognize joined them. He asked them what they were thinking that made them look so sad, and they told him about the crucifixion. Then he began to remind them how it was written in the scriptures that Christ must suffer, and why then had they been afraid? They did not know how to answer; but as they drew near their home, they begged their companion to come in to supper with them. There at the table, when he took the bread and blessed and broke it, suddenly it was as if their eyes had been blind and now were opened. They looked at him and saw that it was Jesus!

Then he vanished, but they were so excited and overjoyed that they went straight back to Jerusalem to tell the disciples what had happened. There they found eleven of the Twelve gathered together—for Judas now was gone—and they heard that the Lord had appeared that day to Peter. And even as they were speaking, Jesus came again into their midst. He showed them the marks of the nails still in his hands and feet, and he told them again that it had been the purpose of God that he should have to suffer and die, and then come back from death.

In the last chapter of the Gospel of John there is an account of how the risen Jesus appeared to the disciples one day when they had gone back to their fishing boats on the lake of Galilee, and of what he said that day to Peter and to John. And in the first letter to the Corinthians it is recorded that he showed himself also to the apostle James, though it is not told how or where.

But the how and where are not what matter most. The wonder of seeing Jesus alive again was so thrilling that the disciples could not always give an exact description of it. The surest witness to the fact that their Master had come back to them was not in what they said but in what happened to them and in them. The men who after the crucifixion had been despairing were filled now with a new certainty and joy. The men who had thought that all their real life was ended saw that the best of it was only now begun. Jesus had told them, "I am with you always, even unto the end of the world." He had told them also, "Go therefore and make disciples of all nations"; and in the days that should begin the history of the early Church, that is exactly what they would go out with eager devotion to try to do.

CHAPTER 3

THE SPIRIT STIRS THE DISCIPLES

N JERUSALEM the disciples and Mary, the mother of Jesus, and other women who had believed in him were met together "in an upper room." It was in an "upper room" that the Gospels tell us the disciples sat down with Jesus for the last supper the night before his crucifixion. So it may have been to this same room that they had come back now, and in the words of the book of Acts they "devoted themselves to prayer."

It was not safe for them to let many people know that they were meeting. It was better to come through the streets one by one so that they would not be noticed. Rulers in Jerusalem who had brought Jesus to his death might be on the watch for those who had been his followers. And once inside the house there must be no loud sounds that those outside could hear. They prayed together and talked in low voices. And part of the time they had no need to say anything at all. Each of them had so much to remember that they could sit still and know that they were all thinking of Jesus.

Mary, his mother, saw him in her memory as he used to be in Nazareth: at first the little boy who went with her to draw water at the village well or watched her as she kneaded leaven into meal; then with his young strength at work in the carpenter shop with Joseph; then the man with the deep eyes that looked at everyone so straight and true, the lips that could speak so lovingly, and the hands that were so quick to help. Even as she had adored him, she had been frightened for him. There was so much in him that she could not understand. He seemed to belong to God so fully that she knew he would never stop to consider the danger that might come to him from people who did not want to think of God. And then it had happened—his leaving Galilee as she had feared he would, his coming to Jerusalem where his enemies were, and the crucifixion. She could not help weeping as she remembered how he hung upon the cross. But in her mind she heard again the words of the captain of the Roman soldiers, astonished at the courage of Jesus on the cross and crying out, "Truly this man was a son of God!" In her heart Mary knew now that it was true. "My son," she told herself, "my perfect son! But more than mine. God's son. God's son, whom no cross could kill."

John also was there, and he had his own thoughts. Everyone knew how close he had been to the heart of Jesus, so close that he was called the beloved disciple. But John remembered a day not long before when he had shown how little he had understood his Master. He and his brother James had been talking together. They told each other that anyone as great and wonderful as Jesus must certainly be aiming at some great glory. He must be intending to make himself king in Israel. So why not take advantage of that? They had gone to Jesus and had said to him, "Master, when you have your kingdom, let us have thrones next to you. One on your right hand and the other on your left." But he had rebuked them both. Hadn't they understood that this was not the kind of kingdom he had come to bring—a kingdom where men snatched for honors? In his kingdom men would love God and forget themselves. Did they want to have places in that sort of kingdom, which could belong only to men who were brave and generous and ready to suffer for what was right?

John remembered, and thanked God, that he and James had said "yes," they did want to belong to that sort of kingdom if that was what it meant to be near Jesus. And there in the upper room, remembering Jesus and how he had loved his disciples even when they disappointed him, it may be that John said in his silent prayer, "Lord, help me be a messenger of your love."

Of course in that same room was Peter, and he also had many memories. One day when Jesus first saw him, Jesus had said to him, "So your name is Simon, Jonas' son. I shall give you a new name. I give you the name Peter, for that means Rock." That was what Jesus had said, but what sort of rock had he been? It filled Peter's heart with shame to tell himself the answer. He had said that he would never fail Jesus, but when a servant girl pointed a finger at him in Caiaphas' court, he had denied that he ever knew Jesus. How could he ever forget the sorrow in the eyes of Jesus when Jesus turned and looked at him that night? He had gone out and wept bitterly. He might have gone out and hanged himself, which was what Judas did. He might have—except for one thing. He believed that even then the love of Jesus would not let him go. "And he never will!" cried Peter. "He is risen, and his spirit will live with us and love us forever. That is what we know!"

Because they believed that, the time soon came when the disciples stopped being cautious. Why should they slip about here and there secretly so that they might not be recognized? Why not let everybody know them for what they were—the disciples of Jesus? That would be dangerous, but what of that? It was time to be daring for his sake.

At the Jewish feast of Pentecost, Jerusalem was crowded again, almost as it had been at Passover. When the disciples were met together, something tremendous happened. Into their minds and hearts there came a great rush of courage and power from God, strong as a wind, real as flames of fire. "It is the Holy Spirit!" they cried. And Peter knew that the Holy Spirit moved him that day to preach.

So out among the crowds in Jerusalem he went. "Men of Judaea and all of you who are in Jerusalem, listen!" he said. Then he went on to tell them of Jesus: of how he had come to show men God's meaning for them all, and of how the wickedness of the world had crucified him. "But this same Jesus," Peter said, "God has raised up. He has broken the power of death, for it was not possible that death should hold such a one as Jesus." And he told them that Jesus, living, would be their Savior from their sins.

Then many of the people were moved, and they asked Peter, "What shall we do?" He told them that they should repent and be baptized in the name of Jesus. Three thousand of them did repent and were baptized. So in the same Jerusalem which had crucified Jesus his Church had begun to grow.

Not only would it grow in Jerusalem. It would spread presently to distant places. Among those who listened to Peter on the day of Pentecost were many who had come from other countries, for before this time great numbers of the Jewish people had gone out and settled in different parts of the wide Roman Empire. They had their synagogues in the cities where they lived, but came back when they could to the Temple in Jerusalem to worship at great festivals like Pentecost. When such as these had heard Peter preach and some of them had been baptized, they would not forget when they returned to their scattered homes. They would carry the news of Jesus with them into many lands.

Meanwhile those who were the followers of Jesus met together in their special way. At first all of them were Jews, as Peter and James and John and Andrew were. They continued to go to the Temple worship, just as all the people of Israel had always done. But also they gathered in their own group, not in public places, but in somebody's house. They met now, not on the seventh day, which was the Jewish Sabbath, but on the first day of the week, Sunday, because that was the day of Jesus' resurrection. They sang hymns and prayed, and they broke bread and drank the wine as Jesus had bidden the disciples do in his last supper with them in the upper room.

That was how it was in Jerusalem. And so it was beginning to be wherever the followers of Jesus were. Little congregations would quietly form in more places than anyone yet could know.

CHAPTER 4

THE BEGINNING OF PERSECUTION

HEN PETER preached of Jesus, many people listened eagerly. But there were others who wanted no such preaching. These were the men who had feared Jesus so much that they had been willing to do anything to get rid of him. Some were the priests, like Caiaphas, who thought Jesus was not strict enough and was too merciful to sinners and to people outside the church of Israel. Some were the traders who had had stalls in the courts of the Temple and had been driven out by Jesus because he said such trading had no right to be in the house of God. They had been afraid of him because they knew he would not let wrong things go on the way they wanted them. And when they had crucified him and thought that was the end of him, they did not want crowds of people to be told that he was alive.

After his preaching on Pentecost, Peter got away safely. But soon afterward he and John were going up to the Temple, and at the Temple gate they saw a lame man who sat there begging. Peter healed the man of his lameness in the name of Jesus; and when an astonished crowd came flocking round, he preached again of Jesus. This time the rulers acted quickly. They had Peter and John arrested and put in jail overnight. The next morning they had them brought before the court, threatened them, and told them never to preach of Jesus in Jerusalem again.

But Peter and John were no longer men who could be frightened. When they were let go, they went back to where the other disciples were gathered and told them what had happened. Then they all sang a hymn and prayed. But they did not pray for safety. They prayed that they might be bolder than ever to speak the word of God.

They would need to be bold now and very courageous. The

danger from those who had made themselves enemies of Jesus was growing greater every day.

There was a young disciple named Stephen. He too preached of Jesus. Some who heard him tried to answer him and were enraged when they saw they could not do it. So they spread false tales about Stephen and about what they said he said, until a mob began to gather.

"That Stephen is a liar against God!" somebody shouted; and others in the crowd took up the cry. Then somebody picked up a stone and hurled it at Stephen, and another, and another. He was struck down; and the mob, gone mad now, did not stop stoning him until they killed him. But some who had heard him preach said that his face was like the face of an angel, and that when he was dying he looked up toward heaven and said, "Lord Jesus, receive my spirit."

Now the whole group of Jesus' followers were in peril. Some of them fled from Jerusalem to other places. But the persecution followed them.

At the edge of the mob who stoned Stephen was a young man named Saul. He had come from the city of Tarsus to Jerusalem to study in the school of the rabbis. He had a fierce loyalty to the Jewish law, which he believed to be in every smallest part the law of God. He had heard that Jesus let the law be broken for the sake of Samaritans and Gentiles, and even of sinners generally. He had heard also that when Jesus had been arrested in the garden of Gethsemane and taken before Caiaphas, the high priest, Jesus had dared to stand there before him and say that he was the Son of God. What was that but blasphemy? For that blasphemy Jesus had been crucified.

Now his disciples were declaring that this same Jesus was Christ. But how could anyone who had been crucified be Christ —the Christ whom the Jewish people had been waiting for through all the long years to be the glorious deliverer of the nation? It was an insult to all the great hopes of Israel to think so. That is the way it seemed to Saul, so he hated everybody who had anything to do with Jesus. Those followers of his who had left

Jerusalem were not going to get away safely. He would see to that.

Saul had the high priest in Jerusalem give him letters to the authorities in other places. The letters said that Saul was acting for the high priest and the council. The authorities were to arrest any disciples of Jesus they could find and hand them over to Saul to bring back to Jerusalem.

No one could tell what might happen, or when. At any hour a knock might come at the door, and rough voices might be heard outside, "We are looking for followers of Jesus of Nazareth. Open the door!"

Chapter 5

THE CONVERSION OF SAUL OF TARSUS

BOUT 150 miles from Jerusalem lay the ancient city of Damascus. To go there was a long journey in the days when travel was no faster than one could go on horseback or by the slower camel caravan. But Saul of Tarsus had heard that some of the followers of Jesus who had fled from Jerusalem were in Damascus. So to Damascus he would go in pursuit of them.

The road from Jerusalem led north across Samaria and through the fertile valley of Esdraelon. Then it curved round the foot of the hills of Galilee. Saul on that Damascus road knew that not far away among those hills was Nazareth, where Jesus had grown up. On this journey to hunt down the disciples of Jesus, Saul must have been thinking of him. And there were more reminders of Jesus when the road dipped down toward the blue waters of the lake of Galilee. There on the lake was the town of Capernaum and the shore where Peter and Andrew and James and John had left their fishing boats that day when Jesus had called them to come with him.

Farther along the lakeshore were other places where Jesus had preached the kingdom of God and healed the sick, and where the people had flocked about him. Other men, sent by the rulers in Jerusalem, had come up into Galilee to watch Jesus then and had scowled at him as he taught. And the face of Saul of Tarsus was hard as he remembered the reports of what Jesus had said and of how in his preaching to the common people he had treated the strict laws of Moses as though they did not matter.

But in a strange way Saul of Tarsus was uneasy. He wanted to have only one conviction in his mind—the conviction that Jesus of Nazareth had denied the faith of Israel, that he had been justly crucified, and that anybody who believed in him must be done away with. That was true, he fiercely told himself. Of

27

course that must be true. But *was* it true? said the whisper of a doubt that he could not keep down.

Saul saw again the face of Stephen as the wild mob was stoning him to death—Stephen who looked up before he died and cried, "Lord Jesus, receive my spirit!" He could remember other faces too—faces of men and women he had arrested. Where did they get that look in their eyes as though they saw something he could not see? Why were they not more afraid of him? Where did they get their courage and their strength? Could it even be that they were right and he was wrong? Could it be—no, he was not going to believe it!—that Jesus *was* the Christ?

On past the lake of Galilee went the Damascus road. Off to the left now could be seen the great shining peak of Mount Hermon, its highest slopes white with snow. But Saul's eyes were not on the mountain. He rode like a man who saw nothing but his own dark thoughts. He and the agents from the high priest whom he had brought with him were not far from Damascus now.

Then something sudden and tremendous happened.

It was as though a great light blazed on the road and stopped Saul in his tracks. And in the sky there was a vision, and from it came a voice. "Saul, Saul," it said, "why do you persecute me?"

"But who are you?" Saul asked, as he stood there shocked and trembling.

Then came the answer, "I am Jesus."

"I am Jesus, whom you are persecuting," the voice went on. And as Saul fell to the ground before the awfulness of being face to face with the risen Jesus, he heard the command: "Rise up. Go into the city. And you will be told what you must do."

When he stood up, Saul found that the blaze of light had blinded his eyes. The men who were with him had to take his hand and lead him.

So Saul came into Damascus in a different way from what he had ever imagined, and as a different man.

There was a disciple in Damascus named Ananias. The word came to him from God that Saul was in Damascus. Besides that, Ananias was told to go to see him.

Ananias could not believe it. Go to see Saul of Tarsus? In his prayers he said to God that surely God could not mean that. He told the Lord that he had heard again and again of all the cruel things Saul had done to the disciples in Jerusalem. And here Saul was in Damascus to arrest more disciples and take them to Jerusalem to be punished. Must he really go to see a man like Saul?

Yes, he was to go. This man who had persecuted the followers of Jesus was to become a servant of Jesus. He would be a preacher of the gospel not only in Israel but to nations whom the Jews called the Gentiles, in great cities and before kings of the earth.

So Ananias went where he had been told that Saul was—at the house of a man called Judas in Straight Street. Ananias told Saul that God had sent him there. He put his hands on Saul's eyes and prayed, and Saul's blindness left him, and he could see again.

Soon after that Saul of Tarsus began to go to the synagogues of the Jews in Damascus, and he preached to them that Jesus was the promised Christ and Savior. Of course the disciples of Jesus were full of wonder and rejoicing when they heard this, but most of the people in the synagogues were furious. Here was the man they had depended upon to put an end to what they thought was a false religion, and now he had gone over to the other side. Well, they would see about that! Some of them got together and laid their plans to kill him.

Saul was in such danger that the disciples knew they must try to get him out of the city. But all the gates were watched. So some of the disciples brought him secretly to a house that was near the city wall, and on a dark night they took him to the top of the wall, and in a sort of basket at the end of a rope they let him down to the ground outside.

He made his way back to Jerusalem and appeared among the disciples there. They were astonished, and most of them were suspicious of him and afraid of what he meant to do. Here was the man who had been their most dangerous enemy, and now he claimed to have been converted. How did they know that he was not coming into their midst as a still more dangerous spy?

They might have shut their doors against him if it had not

been for one greathearted, trusting man. His name was Barnabas. It was said that his name meant "son of encouragement," and that is the sort of man he was. He believed that Saul of Tarsus was really changed, and he stood up for him until the other disciples were persuaded. That was a great day in the history of the Church. For the man who had been Saul of Tarsus was henceforth to be called Paul, and he would preach Christ in countries where Christ had never been preached before.

Chapter 6

A GREAT ADVENTURER FOR CHRIST

EFORE THIS time only those who belonged to the Jewish faith had come into the Church of Jesus. For many centuries it had been believed that God had chosen Israel to be his own people above all the other peoples of the earth. Salvation would be for the Jews, not for Gentiles. But those who remembered Jesus knew that his compassion reached out to all human souls, no matter what name they were called by. So the borders of the Church were bound to widen.

One day a disciple named Philip was on the road that ran south from Jerusalem, when an officer of the queen of Ethiopia, going home, drove past in his chariot. Philip ran after him, because he overheard the officer reading aloud to himself from the book of the prophet Isaiah. And what he read was the passage that had in it these words:

> As a sheep led to the slaughter
> or a lamb before its shearer is dumb,
> so he opens not his mouth.
> . . , justice was denied him. . . .
> His life is taken up from the earth.

The man from Ethiopia could not understand what those words could mean. He wanted to know if Philip could explain them.

Then Philip told him that the prophet had been thinking of the deliverer God would send, who would save men because he himself would be willing to suffer. And then he told him of Jesus and of how it was Jesus crucified who was the Savior. The man from Ethiopia was so moved that he asked Philip whether he could not be baptized. And Philip did baptize him there where a stream of water flowed by the road.

On another day in a house in the city of Joppa, Peter was praying. Like others who thought of themselves as children of Abraham, he had looked down on Gentiles. But this day as he prayed, he saw a vision that made him know this was not the way that God would ever have him feel. At that very moment there came a knocking at the door. When Peter went to the door to open it, he found three men who had come to look for him. They said they had been sent by a Roman centurion in the city of Caesarea. His name was Cornelius. Would Peter go with them to Cornelius' house? Yes, Peter would.

Peter set out with the messenger; and when he came to Cornelius' house, he found that this Roman wanted to hear of Jesus. Peter told him; and when he had finished, Cornelius and all his family were baptized.

So now in the Church that was being built in the name of Jesus there began to be people from other nations. But the great missionary to the Gentiles was to be not Philip nor Peter but the man who had been Saul of Tarsus and now was the apostle Paul. (As the word "disciple" meant a learner, so an "apostle" meant one who was sent out to tell what he had learned.) The first disciples, like Peter and John, were also called apostles now; but Paul would go farther and accomplish more than almost all the others.

After his conversion on the Damascus road and his coming to Jerusalem, Paul had gone back to the city of Tarsus, where he was born. Meanwhile in the great city of Antioch, near the coast of the Mediterranean Sea up north of Damascus, there was a little company of disciples. "One of us ought to be sent to help them and encourage them," said Peter and the others in Jerusalem; and they asked Barnabas if he would go. Yes, Barnabas would; and when he arrived, the first thing he thought was, if only Paul were here! He went to Tarsus to find Paul, and he persuaded him to come to Antioch.

Among all the cities of the Roman Empire, Antioch was the third largest. It covered the plain on both sides of the Orontes River and reached up onto the slopes of a mountain behind. Its central street, with its paved roadway wide enough for horses and chariots, was more than four miles long. On that, and on the many streets that ran from it right and left, were the marble fronts of public buildings, statues and fountains, theaters, temples, and triumphal arches. So rich and splendid Antioch seemed, and so busy was its life, that nearly everybody would have thought the little group of people who believed in Jesus were too insignificant to notice. If anyone asked who they were, the answer was, "Oh, some nobodies who believe in some new Christ. Call them Christians."

That is the way people in Antioch described them, and that was the name by which the disciples of Jesus began to be called from that time on. It meant more than the men of Antioch knew. Christ-ians. Christ's people. They would spread over the world, while splendid Antioch would become before long only a heap of ruins.

The Christians were not satisfied just to keep up their own congregation. Paul and Barnabas had been sent to them. Well, they would give them to others who had not had the chance to know of Jesus. So Paul and Barnabas, after hands had been laid on their heads in blessing, started out from Antioch. And the prayers of the congregation followed them.

At the nearby seaport of Seleucia they went on board a ship that was sailing for the island of Cyprus. John Mark, a cousin of Barnabas, went with them. Before long he turned back; but Paul and Barnabas took another ship to the land that reaches out north of the Mediterranean Sea to join the vast continent of Asia to Europe, and is called on the maps Asia Minor. This too was part of the Roman Empire, and the great stone-flagged roads that Rome had built for its armies and for trade stretched across the country. Paul and Barnabas went from city to city and preached in the synagogues.

Some of those who listened to them were deeply moved and wanted to become disciples of the Lord Jesus. But the stricter Jews could not bear to be told that one who had been crucified was the Messiah, for they had expected that the Messiah would come as a great conqueror. In city after city they rose up furiously and drove Paul and Barnabas out. Once they stoned them, and Paul was so badly hurt that at first he was believed to be dead.

But Paul and Barnabas could not be stopped. They dared to go back again to every city they had visited. In each one they found men and women who in spite of all the danger were ready now to be a Christian congregation. They told them to keep up their courage and never to be dismayed if they had to suffer for the kingdom of God. And at length they returned to Antioch and reported to the church there of all that the grace of God had given them strength to do.

After a while they decided to start out again. But there was one thing about which they could not agree. It was about John Mark, who on their first journey had lost his nerve and turned round and gone home. Barnabas wanted to trust him once more and take him with them. But Paul refused. So Barnabas with Mark went off to Cyprus, and Paul took another disciple, Silas, as his companion.

They two went back to visit the disciples in the cities of Asia Minor where Paul and Barnabas had preached first. In one of those cities a new companion, the young Timothy, joined them. Across all the width of Asia Minor they went, until they came to the port of Troas on the Aegean Sea, which separates Asia from the continent of Europe and the Western lands.

There one night Paul had a dream. In his dream he saw a young man standing on the opposite shore in Macedonia; and the young man was calling, "Come over and help us!" That dream seemed to Paul a sign from God. So a new chapter in the life of the Church began. Paul took a ship to cross the Aegean, this time to carry the gospel to Macedonia and to Greece.

CHAPTER 7

JOURNEY'S END

OW BEGAN the work, carried on in the face of difficulty and danger, that was to plant Christianity among the nations of the Western world.

Paul and his companions came to the city of Philippi. Philippi had been founded as a Roman military colony, but Jews also had settled there. They used to meet for prayer in an open space on a river bank; and when Paul preached to them, some of them were converted; and those few were to grow into a Christian congregation so devoted that Paul afterward loved them in a special way.

But not all the people of Philippi had any use for Paul. Out by the river was a girl who fell into trances and told people's fortunes. Paul brought her back to her right mind. Then her managers, who had made money from the fortunes the girl was supposed to tell, were indignant. They accused Paul to the Roman magistrates, and he and Silas were whipped and thrown into jail. The next day they were let go only because the magistrates found out that Paul belonged to a family who had been honored by being made Roman citizens, and they did not dare to treat a man like that as an ordinary criminal.

Paul and Silas stayed a while longer in Philippi at the house of one of the new Christian disciples. Then they went on to the city of Thessalonica. Many Jews were there also, but most of them were not like those who had welcomed Paul in Philippi. Instead they hated the idea of anyone preaching Jesus as the Christ, just as Paul himself had hated it before he was converted. They stirred up a mob and went yelling to the house of a man named Jason, who had taken Paul in. They dragged Jason before the magistrates and accused him of sheltering this Paul whose preaching was "turning the world upside down." And because

Jason might be in serious danger, Paul and Silas left Thessalonica after they had preached in other towns nearby.

Not long afterward they were met by more violence in the city of Berea, and escaped by ship to Athens. Here was the most famous of all the cities of Greece, and the most beautiful. On its hills the pillars and walls of white marble temples rose against the deep blue sky, and in its streets and open squares were colored and gilded statues and altars to many gods. Also Athens had been for centuries like a great university. Here the men of highest learning gathered, and on Mars Hill they taught and debated every new idea. Paul began to talk to them in their own terms; but when he spoke about the Resurrection, they shrugged their shoulders and turned away. "Talk to us some other time," they said.

Knowing that he had failed at Athens, Paul went on to Corinth. Corinth stood on a plain with a sheer mountain behind it and in front a wide harbor where the ships were moored so thick that their masts were like a forest of trees. Its streets were crowded with sailors and traders from all quarters of the earth, tough and brawling. A hard place to preach in, Corinth seemed. But there were people who welcomed Paul. And at Athens Paul had learned a lesson. He would not try again to match arguments with people who only wanted to play with ideas. He would tell out from his heart the whole story of Jesus. So that was the way he preached in Corinth. "I decided to know nothing among you," he said, "except Jesus Christ and him crucified."

For nearly two years Paul stayed in Corinth, working to support himself and preaching. Toward the end of that time there was a riot against him, as there had been in Thessalonica. But the Roman governor put an end to it; and when at length Paul left Corinth, he left behind him a Christian congregation that would not be destroyed.

Now for a while there was a calmer time. By a roundabout way Paul went back to Jerusalem to worship in the Temple, and then to Antioch to see again the Christians who had prayed for him when he first set forth to preach the gospel.

But more adventures in the name of Christ, and more perils, lay ahead.

Paul made again the long journey through Asia Minor, visiting the churches he had founded. Then he came to magnificent Ephesus, the city at the western edge of Asia Minor where was the famous temple to the goddess Diana. She was supposed to be the protector of the city, and the worship that centered in her temple was what made the city prosperous. Large numbers of men got their living by making little silver images of the great statue of Diana that stood in her temple. After Paul had been preaching for about two years in Ephesus, people stopped buying the images. One of the silversmiths, a man named Demetrius, grew more and more full of sullen anger until one day his anger blazed into action. He began to tell all the other makers of images that their trade was being destroyed. If things kept on as they were going, the first thing they knew the temple of Diana and all her worship would be despised. He threw the whole crowd of silversmiths into an uproar. They poured through the streets and into one of the theaters, shouting, "Great is Diana of the Ephesians!" They caught two of Paul's companions, and they wanted to lay hands on Paul; but when he tried to go into the theater, the Christians in Ephesus prevented him. And when the riot had died down, he went across the Aegean Sea to visit again the church at Philippi and other churches he had founded in Macedonia and Greece.

Once more he returned to Jerusalem, and this time he was to meet violence greater even than he had faced in other cities. When he had gone up to the Temple, a crowd of the more fanatical Jews rushed against him and might have torn him to pieces if he had not been rescued by the Roman centurion who commanded the Temple guard. And more than forty men took an oath together that they would not eat or drink until they had killed Paul.

The centurion then sent him with an armed escort to the Roman governor Felix in Caesarea. Felix kept him in prison, hoping—so it was said of him—that a bribe might be offered if he would set Paul free. But after two years he was removed and a new governor, Porcius Festus, sent by Rome to take his place.

Now Paul had a chance to make his defense against his accusers before Festus and also before the local ruler, Herod Agrippa, whom the Roman had invited to hear what Paul had to say. Then Paul spoke the great story of his life that is recorded in the twenty-sixth chapter of the book of Acts, and in which he told of the appearance of the risen Jesus to him on the road to Damascus. "Whereupon," he said, "I was not disobedient to the heavenly vision."

Both Festus and Agrippa were impressed by Paul's defense, but Paul had already asked that his case might be tried at Rome. "This man could have been set free," said Agrippa, "if he had not appealed to Caesar." But since he had appealed, there was nothing for Festus to do but to send him on. So Paul was put in the charge of a centurion and soldiers who were to take a group of prisoners to Rome across the Mediterranean.

Day after day while the ship plowed through the wide sea, Paul had long hours when his thoughts could go back to what had happened. So many scenes, so many crowded actions, since that night when in his dream he had seen a young man of Macedonia appealing to him to "come over and help us." In those years he had lived through more experiences than most men know in all the years between the time they are born and the time they die. The changing scenes passed before the eyes of his mind like an endless panorama: Philippi, Thessalonica, Athens, Corinth, Ephesus, Jerusalem.

Surely it seemed as though there had been dangers enough. But the tale of them was not finished. Paul had been remembering what happened in the months that were past. Now he had to turn to what was happening on the sea and on the ship.

The clear sky of the first part of the voyage had changed to clouds. The wind shifted from the south to the northeast. It blew harder, until it became a screaming gale. On the mountainous seas the ship was helpless. Off an island it was driven upon a ledge of rock, and the great waves began to smash the hull to pieces. Only after a hard struggle did those on the ship get to shore on broken planks.

Now Paul could add that shipwreck to the perils he had passed through. He summed them up in one of the letters he wrote to the church in Corinth: he had been in prisons more times than he could remember, stoned once, beaten by mobs five times, punished with the Roman scourge three times. He had known what it was to go days and nights without sleep, to be tired and hungry, to be cold and naked. But because of his love for Christ he had not been overcome. "When I am weak," he said, "then I am strong."

It was on the island of Malta that Paul and the centurion and the soldiers guarding him were wrecked. They had to wait there three months before the centurion could get another ship. Then they continued the voyage and at length landed on the shores of Italy.

Along the famous highroad called the Appian Way, Christians from Rome came out to meet Paul. All his life as an apostle Paul had wanted to come at last to Rome. This was the capital of the world. From here the legions had gone out to conquer all the countries of the West. Through its proud streets victorious generals and their armies had staged their triumphs at the end of successful wars: the ranks of the Roman infantry, with the gilded eagles borne before; the rolling of chariots; the glitter of shields and helmets; the magnificence of the emperor himself.

Into this great Rome, Paul came. To the crowd in the streets he did not look like a conqueror. He was a prisoner under guard. But Paul was not discouraged. In Rome, awaiting trial, he still could talk about Christ to all who came near him. He could write letters to the Christian congregations he loved. Some of the letters that he wrote are part of the New Testament now. In them is shown the faith that upheld him even in prison.

"I want you to know, brethren," he wrote to his friends in Philippi, "that what has happened to me has really served to advance the gospel, so that it has become known throughout the whole praetorian guard and to all the rest that my imprisonment is for Christ; and most of the brethren have been made confident in the Lord because of my imprisonment and are much more bold to speak the word of God without fear."

CHAPTER 8

FIRE AND FURY

N THE Western world multitudes of people were thankful for what they called the Pax Romana, which meant the Roman peace. They did not always stop to think of how cruelly sometimes that peace had been created. By continual conquests Rome had subdued the kings and countries that once might have been fighting one another. Now from the island of Britain in the West all the way deep into Asia, and from Europe across the Mediterranean Sea to Africa, Rome was in control. Roman legions would crush any revolt. Roman governors and magistrates kept law and order.

Mostly Rome did not interfere with the religions of the various peoples in the empire. So the many colonies of Jews were free to worship in their synagogues. A strange, stubborn people, the Romans thought they were; but they could be let alone so long as they made no trouble. And at first it was supposed that the Christians were just a special Jewish group who need not be bothered about.

Meanwhile most of the ordinary people in Rome itself and in many of the Roman provinces followed the habits that had been handed down for generations. They went to the temples of the old gods and goddesses: Jupiter, Juno, Mars, Neptune, Venus, and the rest. It was through the favor of those gods that Rome had grown so great, they thought. Therefore anyone who did not do homage to the accepted gods might need to be watched as being perhaps some sort of secret enemy of Rome itself.

Also there was something else that had become almost worship. In temples here and there statues of the emperor had been set up. To bow before the emperor's statue was like saluting the flag. Who would refuse to do it unless he was disloyal?

But now it began to be noticed that these people who were called Christians had strange ways. They would not go to the amphitheaters, where bloodthirsty crowds went to watch the gladiators, men trained to fight one another for the sport of those who looked on, or to see wild beasts let loose on prisoners who had been condemned. They would not worship in the Roman temples. They would not burn incense before the statue of the emperor. The report was that they worshiped some supposed Christ who had also been called their king. And these meetings they had in one another's houses and these secret meals that they called Communion. Who knew what went on then?

Plenty of rumors and tales were spread by people who claimed they knew.

"Better be suspicious of these Christians," one man would say.

"Yes, and with good reason," his neighbor would answer.

"They keep to themselves, and nobody knows what they do when they get together at night."

"They despise the gods. What are they but atheists?"

"They will not reverence the emperor. They could be traitors to the empire."

"Every place would be better off without them. They ought to be driven out."

So the talk went back and forth. Few people troubled to find out the truth about the Christians. False ideas, once started, spread fast. Suspicion led to fear, and fear to anger and to hatred. Violence was not far off.

It broke loose in Rome, not long after Paul had come there.

Much of Rome was built magnificently of stone and marble: the emperor's palace, the senate house, the temples, the great colosseum where the gladiators fought, the forum. But other parts of it, where the poor lived, were built of wood. In those crowded slums and in the market sheds were no broad avenues such as in the other parts of Rome. Instead there were crooked alleys where the houses were huddled close together. If there should be a fire, it would be hard to stop.

On the eighteenth of July in the year 64 fire came. It broke out in the wooden stalls of what was called the Circus Maximus. Once started, it leaped from one cluster of buildings to another. For six days the roaring flames raged across the city. People ran this way and that in a blind panic, for it looked as though all Rome was burning.

Who had started the fire? Who was to blame? Let the people find out, and their passion would be terrible.

Then the whisper began: "It was this emperor of ours who started it! Nero himself set Rome on fire."

The Emperor Nero was known to be vain and selfish and of a savage temper. He had had his own mother murdered. If he wanted anything, there was nothing he would not do to get it. He wanted the whole of Rome to look magnificent, people said. He would get rid of the shabby part of it so that he could build it new. What did it matter to him that what poor people owned should be burned up and some of them burned up with it?

But Nero was as shrewd and crafty as he was cruel. He said that Rome had been set on fire by the Christians. They were the ones who had done it—these people who already had been suspected as enemies of Rome.

So the anger of the crowd went off on another trail.

In what was left of Rome the Christians were hunted. Those who were found were taken to the garden of Nero's palace. Covered with oil, they were tied to stakes and set on fire. Or they were beaten and wild dogs turned loose upon them.

It was at the time of the great fire, or near then, that Paul is believed to have been executed in Rome. And so, it is believed, was the apostle Peter. According to the tradition of the Church, Peter was not only crucified but crucified head down. He said he was not worthy to die in exactly the same way as Jesus Christ, his Master, died.

From that time on all Christians lived in peril. They and their religion were outside the protection of the law. Whenever something roused the crowd against them, or whenever some magistrate chose to start the machinery of punishment, they might be arrested, imprisoned, or even put to death.

CHAPTER 9

CHRISTIANS WHO DARED DEATH UNAFRAID

OR 250 years after Paul had laid down his life for Christ, peril lasted for all Christians. Mostly they had to meet in secret places. In Rome itself they dared to gather only in what were called the catacombs. These were long, dark galleries dug under the ground. There the Christians went for worship, and there they buried their dead.

Sometimes the danger came because some man knew his neighbor was a Christian and determined to accuse him. Sometimes it came because the magistrates had been ordered to hunt the Christians out.

In the city of Smyrna a mob laid hold of the leader of the Christian congregation, the saintly old Polycarp, and dragged him before the Roman proconsul.

"Swear by the fortune of Caesar!" said the proconsul. "Swear, and I will release you. Revile Christ!"

"Eighty years I have served him," Polycarp answered, "and he never did me wrong. How can I blaspheme my king who saved me?"

So because he would not deny his Christian faith, he was tied to a stake and burned to death.

In North Africa one of those who chose to die rather than deny the Lord Jesus was a young woman whose name was Perpetua. She was married, and she had a baby. When she was arrested, what distressed her most was that her baby might be taken from her. But when they let her have her baby with her in the prison, she said, "The dungeon became to me like a palace, so that I preferred being there to being anywhere else."

Her father came again and again and begged her to do what the Roman court demanded. Pretend she was not a Christian. Or at least burn incense to the emperor. Then she might go free.

The Roman Magistrate, whose name was Hilarianus, was not a cruel man. He had to enforce the Roman law, but he did not want to have to send this girl to her death. He tried to persuade her to say something or do something to show that she need not be punished as a Christian. But she said, "I will not sacrifice."

Then Hilarianus asked, "Are you a Christian?"

And very simply she anwered, "I am a Christian."

That settled the matter. They took her, with others who had been condemned, to the arena in the city of Carthage. While the people in the crowded seats looked on, the beasts were let loose from their cages. Perpetua was attacked, but she was not killed. Then one of the gladiators was ordered to go into the arena with his sword. Perpetua showed him where to strike. And with courage to the end she died.

Such were among those who gave their lives for their Lord. Some were persons of high rank, and some were humble people. Some were Roman citizens, and some were slaves. Some were men and women, and some were boys and girls. In the words of the letter to the Hebrews, they dared to be as "strangers and pilgrims on the earth."

The persecution of the Christians was not the same all the time or in all places. Some emperors grew tired of it. One of them might say, "What is wrong with these people? They do not commit crimes. They have done no harm to their neighbors. In fact they are better people than those who are not Christians. Why bother, then, with their strange beliefs? Let them alone."

It even began to look as though all the emperors would feel that way. And then about the year 300 the persecution broke loose again, more terrible than ever.

In the Roman armies of the East one of the men in high command was Diocletian. In 284 he was made emperor. Because he had been a soldier all his life, Diocletian's one idea was that the defenses of the empire should be made safe. There were threats from outside. Persian armies were on the east. On the north the tribes from the wild regions of Germany were continually trying to break through the Roman lines. Therefore no danger must be permitted at home. And the Christians, Diocletian thought,

might be a danger. They would not pledge their loyalty to the emperor and the empire in the same way that other people did. How did he know, then, that they could be depended on if trouble came? It was time that the question between the Christians and the Roman Empire be settled once for all.

More cruel than Diocletian was his son-in-law, Galerius, to whom Diocletian had delegated part of his imperial authority. Galerius now set himself to make sure that through the whole Roman world the edicts against the Christians should be enforced. All persons everywhere must prove that they were not Christians or be liable to be tortured or put to death.

It was a frightful time. Christians were sent to slow punishment in prisons or in the mines or chained to the oars in Roman galleys. Sometimes they were killed, not only singly, but wholesale. In Asia Minor a whole town inhabited by Christians was surrounded by soldiers, set on fire, and the town and the people in it burned. In Rome whatever property the Church had was seized and many of its members killed. In Syria, in Palestine, and in Egypt for year after year there were violence and terror. In faraway Britain a soldier named Alban, who had been in Diocletian's army, gave up his life in trying to protect another Christian who was hidden in his house. As the first martyr of the Church in England, his name belongs to the great old church of Saint Alban's, which stands not far from London.

So the Roman rulers did their utmost to destroy the whole Christian Church. Some Christians were cowed into surrender. They gave up their sacred scriptures to be burned. They cried for mercy. But they were not the real Church, nor most of the Church. The great number faced the persecution and never yielded.

At last in all the Roman provinces the people generally—the people who were not Christians—grew tired of the whole cruel business. Even such a man as Galerius began to know that he was beaten. In the Christian Church he and others like him had come up against a kind of courage that they could not break down. Twenty-five years after the persecution began, Galerius took back the edicts which had been issued. Christians should be free to hold their religious assemblies again. And he wanted them "to pray to their God for the welfare of the emperors, of the state, and of themselves, that the state might prosper in every respect, and that they might live quietly in their homes."

It might have been said already then, as it was said at a time afterward when Christianity was threatened, "The Church is an anvil that has worn out many hammers." By themselves the men and women in the Christian Church were not different from other people. They were not born heroic. But their faith in Christ had made them strong. They could read and remember the words of Jesus in the Fourth Gospel: "In the world you have tribulation; but be of good cheer, I have overcome the world." And they had tried to live by what Paul had written to the church of the Thessalonians. "Encourage the fainthearted, help the weak." They had known that if they kept faithful, they could outlast all persecution. And they did.

CHAPTER 10

AN EMPEROR BECOMES A CHRISTIAN

OW SOMETHING came true that the Christian Church had hardly dared to believe would happen. A man was about to become emperor who not only would stop the persecution of the Church. He would protect it and finally join it himself.

Diocletian, who had been emperor, grew tired and disgusted; and he gave up his crown. He meant that Galerius should succeed him, and Galerius did. But before long war broke out among the leaders of the Roman armies in various parts of the empire. The man who kept gaining in power was the young Constantine, who was backed by the armies of the West. In 312 he marched down into Italy against one of his rivals. There not far from Rome it was said that he saw in the sky a vision of a shining cross surrounded by the words *"Hoc signo vinces"*—"by this sign thou shalt conquer."

To Constantine this meant that he must take the side of the Christians if he would win the battle—the battle of the Milvian Bridge—that was about to begin. He did win that battle. Later he got rid of his other rivals one by one. In about ten more years he had made himself emperor of the whole Roman world.

Before he had thus risen to full power, Constantine had begun to show increasingly that he meant to be a friend to the Christian Church and not its enemy. In what was called the Edict of Milan, in 313, he ordered that everyone should be free to worship according to his own choice. So for the first time to be a Christian was no longer against the law.

Constantine had his children brought up by Christian teachers. He built many churches and gave support to the Christian clergy. And in 325 he brought together the leaders of the Christian Church from all over the Christian world to the city of Nicaea.

He wanted them to put into words what would be the faith of Christians everywhere.

It was hard for those who came to that Council of Nicaea to believe what they saw. There was the Roman emperor in his gold and purple robes coming into a Christian gathering not with soldiers nor surrounded by his guards but as a friend to listen. And in that same gathering were men who had been through the persecution. There was a bishop from Egypt, one of whose eyes had been put out, and another bishop who had been tortured with red-hot irons and was crippled in both hands. Now the persecution was over. There would be no general violence against the Church in the Roman Empire again. And except for the Emperor Julian, called Julian the Apostate, whose short reign lasted only through the two years 361 to 363, the emperors would show favor to the Church.

Near the end of his life Constantine was baptized. When he died, it was almost exactly three hundred years since Jesus was crucified by a Roman governor, Pontius Pilate. On that day his disciples had seemed so few and insignificant that there could be no reason to notice them any more. Much had happened since then.

The first thing that had happened was the spreading of the gospel, not only by apostles like Peter and Paul, but by men and women whose names never got into history. Paul, of course, was the greatest missionary. Largely because of him congregations of new Christians sprang up in most of the important cities of Asia Minor, Macedonia, and Greece. But the Christian Church in the greatest city of all, the church in Rome, had been established and had grown to many members years before Paul came there.

There was an early tradition that Peter founded it. But that is doubtful. More probably no one big person founded it. Because the Roman government had been building great highroads and had made them and the sea safe for travel, ordinary people were continually coming to Rome for business and other reasons. Some of them had heard of Jesus, and they told about him. They brought the gospel, and they spread it, because they knew how

their own lives had been changed by the saving love of God through Jesus.

In the same way the gospel spread to Gaul, which now is France, and to the British Isles; and south of the Mediterranean Sea to the great city of Alexandria in Egypt, and all along the North African coast.

A second thing that happened was the collection of the writings that make up our New Testament. There are the letters that Paul had written to various churches, and letters of John, of Peter, and of other disciples. There are the four accounts of the life of Jesus that stand at the beginning of the New Testament as the Gospels of Matthew, Mark, Luke, and John. There is the book of Acts, which is a history of the first days of the Christian Church. And at the end is the book of Revelation, full of great visions and promises of God's deliverance for Christians when the Roman persecutions had begun.

As the Church by the second century had its Bible, the New Testament added to the Old, so also it began to have a creed. "Creed" comes from the Latin *credo*—"I believe." When anyone became a Christian, he stood up and declared the faith that now he would try to live by. The words were brief, but they were enough to turn a whole life in a new direction. "I believe in God . . . ; in Jesus Christ . . . ; in the Holy Spirit."

That was the beginning of the creed that is recited now by many Christian congregations all across the earth. It was called the Apostles' Creed, because it seemed to sum up what the apostles had taught. The creed is longer than it was at first. The early Church added sentences that said more about Jesus and how he was crucified and rose again, and about the Church and the forgiveness of sins and everlasting life. But in its simplest, shortest words the creed can be the Christian's pledge of loyalty. It is as though each one who recites it were saying: "I believe my life belongs to God, our Father, and so I will give him my obedience. I believe that in Jesus there comes to me the love of God that saves me from my sins. And I believe that the Holy Spirit in my mind and heart will be God speaking there."

Besides the Apostles' Creed there is another and longer one. It is called the Nicene Creed, because it was first drawn up by the leaders of the Church from all countries of the Roman Empire in the council which the Emperor Constantine called together in the city of Nicaea.

It begins:

I believe in one God the Father Almighty; Maker of heaven and earth, and of all things visible and invisible.

And then in its central part the creed goes on to say:

And in one Lord Jesus Christ, the only-begotten Son of God, begotten of the Father before all worlds, God of God, Light of Light, very God of very God, begotten, not made, being of one substance with the Father; by whom all things were made; who, for us men and for our salvation, came down from heaven, and was incarnate by the Holy Ghost of the Virgin Mary, and was made man; and was crucified also for us under Pontius Pilate; he suffered and was buried; and the third day he rose again, according to the Scriptures; and ascended into heaven, and sitteth on the right hand of the Father; and he shall come again, with glory, to judge both the quick and the dead; whose kingdom shall have no end.

Constantine's desire was that the creed should bring the whole Church together into agreement as to the faith that all Christians hold. But before there was any agreement, there was a long, unhappy struggle. It was between one group who rallied behind a spokesman named Arius and another group led by Athanasius. They all agreed that it is through Jesus that we know the truth about God. Athanasius wanted to say—as the creed now does say—that Jesus Christ is "of one substance with the Father." But Arius and those who followed him wanted to say that he was "of *like* substance."

What difference did it make? we might wonder; and what do the words mean anyway? But it did make a difference, and a great difference. For there was danger that what Arius taught might be a watering-down of the Christian faith to make it easier for the pagan peoples to fit it into their own ideas. Christ would be a sort of half-god whom they could accept. But what Athanasius and those who followed him in the Council of Nicaea were trying to say was this: that Jesus was the one life in whom the nature of God is completely seen. He was the goodness of God coming down to take the "form of a servant, and [to be] made in the likeness of men," that every man might look to him and see the power that can save him.

The Greek words and forms of speculation in which the men of Nicaea had to think and speak make their arguments hard sometimes for the thought of a later age to follow. But what they put into the creed was immensely more important than a matter of language. It was a safeguarding of the heart of the Christian faith. For to say that Jesus is "of one substance with the Father" means that God, who might have been the great unknown, is truly known in Jesus. It means that when we remember Jesus, so absolute in righteous purpose, so strong and yet so merciful, we can be sure that that is the way *God is*. We do not have to stop with believing that in *some* ways we can know what God is through Jesus, but that maybe there are other ways in which God is not like Jesus at all. Instead we can know that the heavenly Father will always deal with us as Jesus, the beloved Son, dealt with those he loved and who loved him.

Even the men in the Church who were most supposed to be good were not always good. Some of them could be proud and stubborn when they argued about the creeds. But Jesus himself was more powerful than any argument. As long as people were thinking of him, they had in their hearts something that would make them different from the world around them. The Church had also something more that he had given. It had baptism as the promise of the washing away of sin. In baptism a man or woman or boy or girl was signed with the sign of the cross in token that he should "not be ashamed to confess the faith of Christ cruci- fied." It had the Lord's Supper, or the Communion, with the blessing of the bread and wine, just as Jesus had blessed them in the upper room. As Christians took bread and wine, which repre- sented his body that had been broken and his life given on the cross, his living presence was there with them again.

So the Church had its creeds and its holy ways of dedication and of worship that are called the sacraments. Also it had its ministry. In the beginning the Church depended upon the apostles, such as Peter and John and James and Paul. Then as congregations multiplied, the apostles appointed men who were called presbyters or elders—men who could be trusted for their character and experience to lead the worship and to set an example for the people's lives. One of the presbyters might be called the bishop. By the end of the first century or the middle of the second there was a bishop as head of the Church in nearly every region. When Constantine wanted to have a council that would speak for the whole Church, it was mostly the bishops that he called together. Many of them were learned, and some of them were saintly.

But the Church was something bigger than bishops or any other special group. It was the thousands and ten thousands of men and women all over the Roman world who never would be famous but who showed by their everyday lives what a difference there was in people when they were Christians. In a time when many were corrupt, they kept their habits clean. In a world where there was much cruelty, they were kind. They helped one another in distress. Because they had loved the Lord Jesus and had trusted in God, they had lived up to their best even when times were worst. So it had come true that even their pagan neighbors saw that these Christians who kept on being good and doing good made every neighborhood a better place for everyone to live in.

CHAPTER 11

AMBROSE AND AUGUSTINE

HERE IS an ancient prayer that asks: "In all time of our tribulation, in all time of our prosperity—*good Lord, deliver us.*"

The Church in the time of Constantine needed to say part of that prayer. It had been through tribulation, and now prosperity had come. Or to change the long words into short ones, it had had the Lord's deliverance when everything was hard. Now it needed his deliverance when it looked as if everything would be easy. Tribulation had made Christian men and women brave. But when the times were different, what would they be? Probably not many stopped to ask themselves that. They were just glad not to be persecuted any more.

In the years after Constantine people went into the Church who would not have gone into it before. It was safe now and beginning to be popular, and no longer was there any special courage in belonging to it. A person might be baptized just because that had come to be the expected thing to do.

There was danger too that the Christians might forget to fight against the big things. When all the world was against them, they had to fight—as the words at baptism reminded them— "against the world, the flesh, and the devil." Their business was to try to stop, whenever they could, whatever was mean and wrong and cruel. But now they might begin to think their business was to fight against somebody's ideas that did not seem to them correct.

So the Church grew full of arguments. Men thought that they were contending for the truth, but often it was for little pieces of the truth. When they had been standing up together against the heathen world, they were showing the power of Christ, and that *was* truth. But it was not so good when they kept meeting now in councils and disputing about particular ways to think of

Christ—and driving out as "heretics" those who could not think as most of them did.

The arguments that had been so hot at the Council of Nicaea kept flaring up again. There were churches that called themselves Athanasian and some that called themselves Arian. Sometimes they would have nothing to do with each other—like some churches that call themselves Christian now.

But God has a way of bringing good even out of what has often seemed not good at all. The councils of the Church that were called together in the 150 years after the Roman Empire began to be Christian stirred up hot tempers and ugly quarreling. That was a shame on Christian men, who could have turned to their Bibles and read what the apostle Paul had written, "Let all bitterness and wrath and anger and clamor and slander be put away from you." But at least it was true of them that they were terribly in earnest. And in the councils where the great creeds were written men were trying to think hard and to hand on the faith as fully as they knew how.

Moreover, in the century that began with Constantine, and in the next one, there were some great men in the Church.

One of them was Ambrose. He was governor of the city of Milan in the north of Italy. The bishop there had died, and the assembly was about to meet to choose another. Who would it turn out to be? If Ambrose even thought about it or turned over in his mind this name or that, it is certain that he never thought of the name that presently he was to hear.

He was a strong man and a good man, but he was not responsible for the Church. He had not even been baptized. He was going to the assembly because he was the governor, and he wished to see that there should be no disturbance at the election.

When he came into the assembly and the people recognized him, suddenly a voice rang out, "Ambrose! Ambrose for bishop."

It was like a spark that kindled a fire and swept through the whole assembly. Other voices took up the shout, "Yes, Ambrose! Ambrose for bishop."

Almost before Ambrose could speak, they had elected him. He tried to refuse. How could he who had not even been baptized be a bishop? But the people knew what kind of man he was: strong and true and a Christian at heart. So he was baptized and ordained to the ministry and then made the bishop of Milan.

He became one of the great preachers of the Church. He wrote hymns too and taught the people to sing them. And as a bishop he was afraid of no one.

The emperor then was Theodosius. In the city of Thessalonica there was a famous driver in the chariot races who was a favorite with the people. He was arrested for a crime. The people wanted him in the races all the same, and some of them in angry excitement killed the emperor's officer who had put him under arrest.

Theodosius heard of that, and a cold rage possessed him. So the people had taken their chariot driver? Well, they should see what would happen at their races.

Seven thousand people were in the amphitheater when the races began. Theodosius sent soldiers to block up every gate by which they might come out. Then other soldiers went in with drawn swords to kill everyone they could lay hands on.

Some time after that Theodosius came to Milan. He, the emperor, would go to worship in the cathedral, and everybody of course would make way for him. But he was wrong.

At the entrance to the cathedral stood Ambrose.

"You come with blood upon your hands," he said to Theodosius. Although Theodosius was the emperor, he should not be admitted into the house of God until he had confessed his guilt and sought forgiveness.

And the emperor had to yield. He did confess and pray to be forgiven. A vast change had come since the emperors were pagan. Now an emperor who had authority on earth stood in awe of the bishop, who he believed possessed authority from heaven.

More important for the history of the Church than Theodosius was another man who had to do with Ambrose. This was the young Augustine, from North Africa. His father was not a Christian, but his mother, Monica, was a devoted one. Her love and faith in Augustine held firm even while he was wander-

ing off into sins of which afterward he would be bitterly ashamed. Impatient at home, Augustine had come to Rome and then to Milan. It was like an answer to Monica's prayers when Augustine began to go to hear Ambrose preach, and not long afterward he was suddenly converted. He went back to North Africa a changed man, to give his life to the service of God. Before long he was made a bishop.

Through all the fifteen hundred years since he lived and died, the Church has felt the influence of the books he wrote, and particularly of two. One is his *Confessions,* which laid bare the story of his early life and what it meant to him to become a Christian. The other is *The City of God.*

In *The City of God,* Augustine helped the people of his world —and in all the Christian world since then—to find their faith in God in troubled times. As his life moved on toward its later years, he looked out on events that seemed to mark the end of everything men had been accustomed to. For many centuries Rome had seemed the center of the earth. It was Rome that kept the peace, Rome that preserved law and order, Rome that had made the Western countries civilized. But the power of Rome had been weakening. Little by little the frontiers defended by its armies had been pushed back. Fierce tribes from the north of Europe—barbarians, as the Romans called them—were pressing their attack. And then the unbelievable happened. Alaric, the Goth, with his horde of warriors broke through the defenses, swept down through Italy, captured the imperial city. Rome, which had been the mistress of the world, had fallen.

What could men trust in now?

Augustine gave the answer. Earthly kingdoms and empires, he said, might rise and flourish and pass away. No earthly power could endure forever. But there was another city that had eternal foundations. It was the city of God, which is the Church. In that the souls of men could find their refuge and their home. This was his message, and the world needed it desperately when Rome fell and through the long, dark times that followed.

CHAPTER 12

WHEN MEN DESPAIRED OF THEIR WORLD

HEN THE Roman Empire was still powerful, the Emperor Constantine had built a great new city in the East and called it Constantinople. He preferred to live there and to make the new city the capital from which he ruled.

Little by little what had been the wide Roman Empire began to separate into two parts. The emperors in Constantinople were concerned mostly with the countries to the east. Their wars were against the armies of Persia; and when they were victorious, they grew rich and made Constantinople more splendid than before. The most famous of their buildings was the magnificent church of St. Sophia.

But the emperors in Constantinople paid less attention to the West. Now that they did not live in Rome, they did not care so much as before what happened to it. And even if they had cared more, the time had passed when they could surely protect it.

For the barbarian tribes were breaking through into Italy more and more. After Alaric the Goth there came invaders still less civilized and more savage. These were the Huns. Swarthy men, speaking a language that Europe had never heard, they had ridden on their tough little horses out of the plains of Asia, spreading terror as they came. From the region in Europe that was afterward called Hungary they had attacked and plundered cities in northern Italy. And now in 452 under their chieftain Attila they were advancing on Rome.

Who would protect the city now? No emperor was there. No earthly power was left to stand in the barbarians' way.

Then before the eyes of the astonished Huns appeared a figure such as they had never seen before. It was Leo, afterward called Leo the Great, bishop of Rome. Out to where the Huns were encamped he came in all his churchly robes. The half-naked tribesmen looked at him with a kind of superstitious awe. They were not afraid of any ordinary person. But here was someone who bore himself as though he had an authority that was unearthly.

Attila let himself be halted. He took a great ransom, but he spared the city. The bishop had saved Rome.

It was no wonder that people began to have a new reverence for the head of the Roman Church. He seemed to have the importance that the emperor once had had. And he had a greater importance too. If the emperor had been there, he might have saved the people from the Huns. But he could not show them how to save their souls, or point the way to heaven. The Church could. And in a world that seemed breaking up around them, men craved an authority that they believed held the keys to heaven instead of hell.

There were other great cities in the world: Constantinople, Antioch, Jerusalem, Alexandria. Each one of those had its bishop. But all of them were in the East. In the West there was no bishopric that could rival that of Rome. Many causes, then, combined to increase its authority. Other churches began to turn to the Church of Rome for counsel and for decision in disputed matters. And Leo the Great had made the claim that the bishop of Rome had authority by right. The Church in Rome, he said, had been founded by the apostle Peter—though almost certainly that was not so. He was the first of the apostles, and Jesus had said that he should be the rock on which the Church was founded. All the bishops of Rome were the successors of Peter, said Leo, and therefore they inherited the powers that the Lord had given to him. The bishop of Rome began to be called the pope, which means the Holy Father.

While this special authority of the bishop of Rome was growing, something also was happening that would influence all the life of the Church. The world seemed to be going from bad to worse. Where the barbarians came, old ways of life were broken up. The times were evil, and many men lost hope. They began to feel that the only thing to do was to leave everything they had been accustomed to and spend the rest of their lives in fasting and prayer.

Already there had been examples that could be followed. In Egypt, especially, some of those who had grown weary of the world had gone out to live alone in the desert. One of the first and most famous was a young man named Anthony. His parents had died and left him their possessions. Then one day he was listening to a reading of the Gospels, and in the reading that day were the words that Jesus spoke to a rich young ruler who came to him and asked him what he could do to win eternal life. "Sell what you have, and give it to the poor, and let your treasure be in heaven," Jesus had said to him; "and then come and follow me."

"That is what I will do," said Anthony. And that is what he did. He sold his property; and he went out into the valley of the Nile River, where one could live outdoors with very little shelter and have enough food from the grains that grew on a small piece of fertile ground. Bread and water were enough for him, and he slept on the bare earth. This was before the time of Constantine; and in the great city of Alexandria, Christians had been arrested and put to cruel punishment in the Roman persecution. Anthony went wherever he could to help them and was ready to suffer in their place. The fame of him grew and spread, for here was a man—the people saw—who never indulged his body and was concerned only for his soul. Crowds came to see him and to beg for the prayers of this holy man of God. And when he went still farther off into the desert, disciples followed him and found separate shelter in caves near where he was and tried to fast and pray and discipline their bodies as they saw him do.

Anthony and those who patterned after him were solitary men. It was thought that the more alone they were, the holier they must be and the more devoted to God. But actually it was not good for men to wall themselves off in separation. Shut in to themselves, they could become twisted and queer. If they wanted to leave the world, they still could have a new sort of world together. So gradually it happened that those who had left their old surroundings for the sake of God made centers for their new life in communities. These centers were called monasteries, and the men in them were called monks.

Often the monks were called also the "religious." It was the duty of everyone to try to be good, but ordinary people looked with reverence at the men who had gone into the monasteries and taken there the monks' vow of lifelong poverty, chastity, and obedience. People thought that these were the only ones who had followed the call of religion all the way.

There were great men among those who made monasticism grow and spread.

One of these was Jerome. Late in his life he went from Rome to Bethlehem, and there in the little town where Jesus was born he founded a monastery. He was a man not only of prayer but of great learning also. The books of the Old Testament had been written in Hebrew and those of the New Testament in Greek. But the language of most of the Roman world was Latin. So Jerome took the whole Bible and made a translation of it that was called the Vulgate, which meant that it was in the language of the ordinary people. And for many centuries in the monasteries and in other places the Bible as Jerome had translated it could be read by men who no longer could read Hebrew or Greek.

Another great man was Martin, afterward called St. Martin. He was a soldier in one of the Roman legions in Gaul, which now is France. The story is that one winter day he met a beggar, cold and shivering. He took his cloak, cut it in half, and put half of it round the beggar. That night in a dream he saw Christ wearing the cloak that he had given to the beggar; and he heard Christ's voice saying to him that, when he had clothed the beggar, it was as though he had clothed Christ himself.

After that Martin left the army and became a monk. Later he was made a bishop, but always he was humble and never looked for honors for himself. It was said of him that "he condemned none and never returned evil for evil. Nothing was in his mouth except Christ, nothing in his heart but piety, peace and pity."

But the man who had most to do with the growth of monasticism was born a century later, in 480. His name was Benedict.

In his youth he had gone to Rome to study. But life in Rome

ROMAN EMPIRE
A.D. 400

SCALE OF MILES

0 100 200 400 600

Caspian Sea

PERSIA

Huns

Alans

Ostrogoths

Slavs

Visigoths

Vandals

Lombards

Black Sea

Constantinople

PONTUS

Nicaea

ASIA

Ephesus

THRACE

DACIA

Antioch

Jerusalem

Alexandria

Cyrene

EGYPT

Thessalonica

MACEDONIA

ILLYRIA

ROME

ITALY

Milan

Alemans

Franks

Saxons

GAUL

Northmen

North Sea

BRITAIN

London

Iona

SPAIN

Carthage

Mediterranean Sea

Atlantic Ocean

seemed to him careless and wicked; and he went away—as Anthony had done in Egypt—to be alone and to think of God and pray. Others gathered round him; and presently he was made the abbot—which means the spiritual father—of a nearby monastery. Later he built the most famous of all monasteries, Monte Cassino, not far from Rome. And there he developed what was called the Benedictine Order, a fellowship of monks and a rule for their daily living that was to be followed in monasteries throughout Europe for centuries to come.

Benedict wanted his monks both to worship and to work. Every three hours they met in the chapel to chant the psalms and to pray. When they sat down to their meals, they were to keep silence and listen while one of them read aloud from some sacred book. And there were other hours when each of them was to go to his own place for his private prayers.

Thus they were taught to lift up their thoughts to God. But they were not to be idle with their hands. Some were to cultivate the fields where the food was raised that fed the monastery. Others had duty in the bakeshop and the kitchen. Others worked in the library, copying by hand manuscripts of the Bible in those days when there were no such things as printed books.

Thus the Benedictine monasteries were like little islands of life and light in a world that seemed in many places to be sinking into darkness. The civilization that Rome had built up was breaking down now that the Goths and Vandals and other barbarian tribes had sifted in everywhere. The far-stretching Roman roads were allowed to crumble. The great aqueducts that the Romans had built to bring water to the cities fell into disrepair. Schools had been destroyed. Fewer people and poorer ones were in the villages and towns. The wilderness began to creep back upon what had been the cultivated land. Peasants in their hovels could hear at night the howling of the wolves.

Men felt a little safer when they could see on some hilltop or in a clearing of the forest the buildings of a monastery and know that in some special need they might knock at its gates and find shelter behind its walls.

CHAPTER 13

MISSIONARIES OF THE GOSPEL

T WAS by the monks more than by any others that the new peoples who had come into Italy, and into the countries that now are France and Germany and Austria, and parts of the British Isles, were made Christians. These peoples were the tribes that had fought their way down from the forests of northern Europe or had come in their pirate ships along the coast of the western sea.

They were pagans who had never heard of the Christian gospel until they broke through into the lands that had been ruled by Rome. By the time when the monasteries began to be built, some of them were changing from their pagan ways. But many of them had still not been converted, and some who were supposed to have been converted had a great deal more to learn. So there was need for men filled with the love of Christ to dare go out and preach the gospel where their going would mean hardship and danger too.

In the island of Britain there had been Christians from very early times. No one knows who first carried the gospel there. Perhaps it was some Christian soldier in the Roman armies, or some other Christian who had to go there and did not lose the chance to tell of Christ. As long as the Roman legions were kept in Britain, the number of Christians increased. But when the barbarians began to break the defenses of the empire, the legions in Britain were called home. Then fierce invaders from the coasts of Europe, in their long slender ships driven by sails and banks of oars, landed on the British beaches and fought their way across the country. They killed the people in their way and took possession of the towns. The Christians in Britain were driven to the west into the mountains of Wales.

There in Wales was a lad named Patrick. His father and

66

mother were Christians, and so was he. Something was about to happen to him that seemed at first to be altogether dreadful and yet would make him glorious.

Off the coast of Wales lies the Irish Sea. Over its rough waters and out of its gray mists there came one day the sudden sharp prow of a pirate ship. Men tumbling out of it as it touched the shore caught Patrick and carried him off to Ireland.

There in Ireland he was set to tending the flocks and herds of a tribal chief. After about six years he escaped on a ship that was bound for Gaul. He found shelter in monasteries until at length he was able to make his way back to the home from which he had been carried off.

But he was not to stay there. One night in a dream he seemed to see a company of people across the sea on the shore of Ireland. They cried to him, "We pray thee, holy youth, to come and walk again amongst us as before."

Patrick would go back—back to the land to which he had been taken before as a slave. First he returned to Gaul, to study and prepare to be a messenger of the gospel. Then he went to Ireland, to spend the rest of his life there.

Boldly he challenged the pagan people at their festivals. Once he broke down a famous idol. He gathered Christian congregations and made them strong in the knowledge that they belonged to a great Christian fellowship that reached all the way to Rome. He built a monastery at Armagh, and Irish monks would afterward carry the gospel to other lands. He seemed so great a man of God that his name has come down in history as St. Patrick, the special saint of Ireland.

In our hymnbooks, translated into English words, there is a hymn that tradition says Patrick wrote. Whether or not he was the writer, it puts into words the faith that made him brave and strong:

> I bind unto myself to-day
> The power of God to hold and lead,
> His eye to watch, His might to stay,
> His ear to hearken to my need,

> The wisdom of my God to teach,
> His hand to guide, His shield to ward;
> The word of God to give me speech,
> His heavenly host to be my guard.

After Patrick the next famous saint who belonged to Ireland was Columba. He established one monastery after another, and he built them when he could within sight and sound of the sea. His desire was, as he himself wrote,

> That I might see its heaving waves
> Over the wide ocean,
> That I might hear the thunder of the crowding waves
> Upon the rocks.

He not only looked at the sea. He went out upon it. With twelve disciples he sailed from Ireland to carry the gospel to Scotland. They landed on the little island of Iona, which lifts its rocky cliffs out of the stormy waters close to the Scottish coast. There Columba built a church and a monastery that would make the island seem so holy that for centuries pilgrims would come to it, and the bodies of many kings would be brought there to be buried.

Crossing from Iona to the mainland, Columba converted the pagan king who then ruled the north of Scotland, and many thousands of his people. He converted them not only by the words he preached but by the life he lived. For men saw that here was a man who obeyed the words of Jesus, "Thou shalt love the Lord thy God with all thy heart and mind and soul and strength, and thy neighbor as thyself."

When he knew that his life was drawing to an end, he went up on a hill above the monastery and gave it his farewell blessing. That evening he was writing out one of the psalms. He came to the words, "They who seek the Lord shall lack no manner of thing that is good." He looked up and said that he did not need to write any more. When the bell began to toll at midnight, he rose in haste and went into the church to pray. The monks coming in with lights found that he had fallen before the altar, and one of them raised his head and took him in his arms. As the saint breathed out his life, they said of him that his "face remained so ruddy and wonderfully gladdened by the vision of angels that it seemed not to be that of one dead, but of one living and sleeping."

About the time when Columba and other monks from Ireland were bringing the gospel to Scotland in the north, other missionaries were bringing it back to England in the south. There they came not from Ireland but from Rome.

In Rome a great and good man was bishop. His name was Gregory, afterward to be known as Gregory the Great. He had been a monk before he was elected pope. Heavy duties pressed upon him, for the plague raged in Rome, and invaders called the Lombards threatened the city from without. But Gregory could think also of something bigger than the dangers round him.

One day he passed by the market in Rome where slaves were put up for sale. Among them were some boys, fair-haired and blue eyed. They had been captured from one of the northern tribes that had invaded Britain.

"Who are they?" asked Gregory.

"They are Angles," was the reply.

"They look more like angels," said Gregory.

He could not bear to think that boys like those, and the people from whom they came, might never have heard of Christ. He determined that someone must go to carry the gospel into that part of the island of Britain which, because the Angles had invaded it, had come to be called Angle-land, or England.

The man he chose was the monk Augustine—not the great Augustine who had been a bishop in North Africa nearly two hundred years before, but of the same name. With a band of other monks as companions he set out on the long journey up through Italy, across the whole width of Gaul to the end of the land, and over a stormy arm of the sea to England.

If Gregory had not been so determined, Augustine and his monks would have turned back. For their way was full of hardships: bleak mountains to be crossed, endless miles of slow travel

over narrow tracks through the deep forests, rivers to be forded, danger from wild beasts in the darkness and from suspicious people in lonely villages when they knocked for shelter as the sun went down. And if they should get to England at last, what then? Christians there had been killed before by the pagan peoples. That might happen again.

But Augustine and his companions pressed on. When they did finally set foot on English shores, they found that there was not such danger as they had feared. Ethelbert, the king of the Kentish country in southeast England, where they had landed, had married a princess who was already a Christian. Because of her the king listened to Augustine, and soon he and many of his people were baptized. Near the place where Augustine preached there was built afterward the great cathedral of Canterbury, which stands there to this day.

Augustine and his monks carried the gospel up from the south of England while Columba and his followers were preaching in the north. Before long all England was beginning to be a Christian land.

Also there went out from England a monk who was to do more than anyone else to plant the Christian Church in Germany. His name was Winfrid. Afterward he was to be called St. Boniface. Without fear of danger he went into the dark German forests, where the pagan tribes worshiped Wotan and their other gods with cruel sacrifices. There was a huge oak tree that was sacred to Wotan, and the pagan worshipers believed that the god would strike anyone dead who troubled it. Boniface took an axe and cut the great tree down. He was not struck dead. Instead of that the great tree crashed and split in pieces, and out of it Boniface built a chapel where he could preach the love of Christ.

He converted great numbers of the people and built monasteries from which the work he had begun would be carried on. He never stopped to think of danger. At length some of those who hated him attacked him and killed him with their swords.

He had gone out not to hurt but to help. He was a fighter not against people but against the ignorance and evil from which they needed to be set free. He was the sort of servant of Christ who can be remembered when the hymn is sung:

> For all the saints who from their labors rest,
> Who Thee by faith before the world confessed,
> Thy Name, O Jesus, be forever blest.
>   Alleluia!
>
> O may thy soldiers, faithful, true, and bold,
> Fight as the saints who nobly fought of old,
> And win with them the victor's crown of gold.
>   Alleluia!

CHAPTER 14

MORE DANGER FOR
THE CHRISTIAN CHURCH

INCE THE time of Constantine, who moved his capital from Rome to his new city of Constantinople, the eastern and western halves of what had been the one Roman Empire had been drifting apart. Constantinople was as far away as any place could be from the center of the empire Rome had ruled. It was at the extreme eastern edge of Europe, separated only by a narrow strait from the shores of Asia. The language spoken there was Greek, while in the West men continued to speak Latin. Only in name was the Eastern empire Roman. As time went on, even that name faded away; and the government in the East came to be called the Byzantine Empire—from Byzantium, the name of the ancient town that had stood where Constantine had founded the new city that he called Constantinople.

Constantine's first successors were not as strong as he had been. Even if they had had more ability than they did have, it would have been hard to keep control over the lands to the West. In the year 476 the last official who ruled in the name of the emperor was driven out of Italy when the barbarian invaders captured the city of Ravenna. When that happened, men knew that the old days of the greatness of Rome were gone.

Fifty years later there did arise an emperor who seemed able to win back some of the rule that had been lost. This was the Emperor Justinian. His armies marched to victories in Italy, North Africa, and Spain. Meanwhile he made Constantinople and other cities magnificent with new palaces and public baths, monasteries and churches. The church of St. Sophia, which Constantine had built, had burned down. Justinian brought together ten thousand workmen to rebuild it, and for over five

73

years he watched over them as they created the church that after fourteen hundred years remains as one of the most beautiful structures on the earth—with its interior pillars of colored marble and its walls and the curve of its great dome lined with marble and gold mosaics.

Another act of his made Justinian's name remembered. He assembled what is known as the Justinian Code. This was a bringing together of Roman laws that he hoped would govern both the empire and the Church. But in the end his hope was to fail. The empire was fated to break up. And differences were growing between the Church in the East and the Church in the West that would lead finally to separation of the two.

The Church in the East had had men of great learning and some who were saintly in their lives. One of the most famous was John, the bishop of Constantinople shortly after the time of Constantine, who was called John Chrysostom—the golden-mouthed. He was one of the greatest preachers of all time, and the people loved and honored him because he dared to preach against the sins of emperors and empresses as plainly as he preached to the common folk. But there were not many like him, for generally the emperor could manage to control what bishops and priests and monks might do or say.

The councils of the Church, beginning with the council that Constantine had called at Nicaea, were all in the East. In these councils the bishops and other leaders of the Church from all quarters of the empire had come together to try to put into words the Christian faith about God and Christ and the Holy Spirit, and about the Church and its gospel of salvation. The church in the East called itself the Orthodox Church, by which it meant the church of the right beliefs. Its head was the bishop—or, as he was called, the patriarch—of Constantinople. And its great concern was to hold exactly to what the councils had declared.

In the West the Christian congregations looked more and more for leadership to the bishop of Rome, who now was called the pope. The popes had begun to claim that they were the successors of the apostle Peter and that they had more authority than any other bishop, including the patriarch. The church of Rome called itself the Catholic Church. But that was a name not fully true. For the word "catholic" means "as wide as the world," and the church that had its center in Rome was not that.

Thus the Christian Church as a whole had differences and the beginning of division. These could result in weakness if some new danger should come to the Christian countries. And now that danger was at hand. For in Arabia a new religion was arising.

Arabia is a country that is almost all one vast desert of trackless sand. Untamed tribes, moving here and there on their camels or their swift Arabian horses, were continually at war with one another. But there was one city, named Mecca, to which the many tribes would come on sacred days of the year; and for those days they had to lay aside their weapons and keep the peace. They came to worship in the Kaaba. This was a building that sheltered a great black stone that was believed to have fallen from the sky. And round the stone was a circle of idols.

In Mecca there grew up a young man named Mohammed. He had been a poor camel driver. But a rich widow named Khadija hired him to manage the caravans that she sent out with goods to trade. He did so well that Khadija married him, and it looked as though Mohammed would have only a comfortable and quiet life.

But when Mohammed remembered the idols that his people worshiped, he was troubled. Sometimes he would go off alone to a cave in the wild, rocky cliffs and stay there to think and to pray. And one day he had a vision of the angel Gabriel. The angel told him that he was to be a prophet, a man who speaks for God.

Mohammed saw that idols were no real gods. They were nothing but wooden images. "You rub them with oil and wax, and the flies stick on them," he said. His people must learn that there was One who was mightier, and they must worship him.

In his journeys with the caravans Mohammed had met Jews and Christians. The Jews had learned from great men like Abraham and Moses, and the Christians had Jesus. But Mohammed said that his visions had told him that he was to be a teacher greater than anyone who had gone before. So he began to preach in Mecca, "There is one God, and Mohammed is his prophet."

At first hardly anyone would listen to him. Khadija did. "She believed in me when I was poor and despised," Mohammed said. Little by little a few others followed him.

But mostly the people in Mecca only laughed at him. And some of the men of his own tribe began to hate him. They were guardians of the Kaaba, where the Black Stone and the idols were. Mohammed was not going to break up the old ways of worship if they could help it.

Mohammed had to disguise himself and hide. At length he had to get out of Mecca altogether. He fled to the city of Medina, two hundred miles away. That was in the year 622; and all Mohammedans think of it as a new beginning in history, and call Mohammed's flight the "Hegira."

Until then Mohammed had tried to win followers by persuasion. They were to believe in one God, who created everything and whose will must govern all the life of men. "Islam," he said—which means "submit yourselves to God."

His followers must drink no wine. They must pray five times a day. They must give a tenth of what they had to help the poor. And they must live by the laws that Mohammed the prophet gave them. Those laws were written down and became the sacred book for all Mohammedans. It is the Koran.

But persuading people began to seem too slow. If people would not listen, they must be made to listen. Those who did gather round Mohammed were accustomed to the raids and fighting that had always been the life of the desert tribes. Now with Mohammed leading them, they would fight to make all Arabia accept their prophet.

It was a wild, fierce struggle. Some of the tribes did not want to give up their idols. But the followers of the new prophet were terrible in battle; for Mohammed had told them that if they were killed when they were fighting under his banner, they would go straight to heaven. Mecca was captured. Resistance anywhere else was smashed. Believe Mohammed, live by the Koran, or else die by the sword. That was the choice the tribes in Arabia had.

Ten years after the Hegira, Mohammed died. But the force he had let loose was only in its beginning. "There is one God, and Mohammed is his prophet" was the war cry of Arab armies that rode out on their camels to the north and west. They captured Jerusalem. They took Damascus and made a dreadful slaughter of its people. They overthrew the empire of Persia. They took the proud city of Alexandria in Egypt and burned its famous library. "If its books agree with the Koran," said Omar, the Arab general, "there is no need of them. If they disagree, they are evil and ought to be destroyed."

The Mohammedan advance went on. The Arab armies swept across North Africa. They crossed the Strait of Gibraltar into Spain. They conquered Spain and threatened France. It looked as though the wild camel riders from the desert were about to take possession of all Europe.

But at length in a great battle at Tours, in France, they were defeated. The Mohammedan invasion, which had been like a rising tide about to drown the Christian countries, had begun to ebb.

Yet this did not mean that the world would be as it had been before. There were vast spaces conquered by the Mohammedans that they still ruled. Among these was what all Christians thought of as the Holy Land. That land where Jesus had lived, and Jerusalem where he was crucified, were in the hands of the followers of Mohammed. On the hill in the center of Jerusalem had stood the Temple that was the shrine of worship for the Jews of all the world. In that Temple Jesus had taught. Now it was destroyed. And in its place the Mohammedans had built for their worship a great new building, named after one of the successors of the prophet and called the Mosque of Omar.

Most of the Christian congregations in the invaded countries had disappeared. What would happen to the Christian Church would depend now on whether Christians in other lands could keep the faith through times that were very hard.

CHAPTER 15

THE DARK AGES

HE FIVE HUNDRED years and more after the breakup of the Roman Empire were the worst times that men in Europe ever had to live through. It is no wonder that they are called in history the Dark Ages.

People needed some great influence to bring them courage. The Church was their main reliance, and the Church did give them help. Bad as the times were, they would have been worse without it. But the Church, like everything else, had been weakened by the violence and confusion which had come upon all the life of Europe.

Many of those who were most religious had given up hope of making conditions any better. They began to think that the end of the world might be near. So—as we have seen—great numbers went into the monasteries, where they believed that they could separate themselves from the affairs of this world and by obedience in fastings and prayers make themselves ready for heaven. Some of the monks, as we have also seen, were not satisfied with that. Their devotion made them go out as missionaries to pagan tribes. But for the most part the men who had become monks were moved more by the hope of saving themselves than by concern for the ordinary people in the communities from which they had come. The monasteries became like little islands where some light burned—the light of learning as well as of faith. But very little of that light reached out into the ignorance of common folk in the villages and towns.

Also there was this other fact. In the earlier centuries Christianity had been preached among people who were mostly civilized and knew the meaning of law and order and good behavior. But the tribes who had come down as invaders from the forests of the north and were mixed in now with the population had their own untamed ideas. They had lived by fighting and violence, and the gods to whom they had brought their sacrifices under their sacred oak trees and at other dark altars in the forests were violent and cruel gods. The Christian gospel was a long way from anything they had ever heard of.

In the face of all these difficulties the priests and preachers in the village churches did the best they could. Often they had hardly any more education than the people generally. But they knew the Ten Commandments, and they could preach to the people about obeying those. And they could warn them also against what the Church began to list as the "seven deadly sins," which were pride, envy, greed, luxury, gluttony, anger, and despair.

Certainly those are sins that need to be avoided. If anyone is full of pride, it means that he thinks he is already so much better than other people that there is no reason for him to be any different; so he falls into the deadly error of supposing that God must be satisfied with him as he is. If anyone, on the other hand, is envious, his envy can keep him from making the best of himself, because he is full of the bitter thought that what belongs to somebody else ought to have belonged to him instead. And greed and luxury and gluttony—it is clear what they can result in. Those who are always trying to get more possessions, and to have everything around them soft and comfortable and luxurious, before long are soft and flabby themselves. And if gluttony makes a man stuff his body with food and drink, he can grow more like a pig than like a human being.

If sermons on pride and luxury were preached to kings and princes, as John Chrysostom in Constantinople did preach, then they struck at sins where they really were. And some of the monks needed to hear sermons on some of the other seven sins. As money was given to the monasteries, there were greedy abbots and fat monks who were gluttonous and tempted to drunkenness besides. But there would have been an unreal sound in any sermons preached to the common people on gluttony or luxury. Mostly they lived in wretched poverty and seldom had enough to eat.

But they could understand it when preachers talked about

anger and about despair. Especially about despair. They lived in what seemed not only a hard world but a haunted world. They believed in demons and in witches and in evil spirits that hovered in the air. One of the old chronicles tells of a person who was going to a town where a man was sick. When he got there, the man was dead. Then he remembered that as he was coming along the road, he had seen seven black crows flying; and he said they were seven devils coming to carry off the man's soul. People who had beliefs like that needed to hear about the power of God, and the love of God, for this life and the next.

After death, said the preachers, there will come God's judgment. None of the people, high or low, should be allowed to think that right or wrong made no difference. At the judgment the sinners should be punished for their sins, but those who had tried to be good and were sorry for what they had done wrong would be blessed. The first might be last, and the last first. In that message at least the Church's preachers were true to the spirit of Jesus, who cared for the poor and needy and said, "Fear not, little flock, for it is your Father's good pleasure to give you the kingdom."

But how could people get rid of their sins and hope for the blessing of God? The answer of the Church was clear. Be baptized. Confess your sins to the priest. Come to church and listen to the saying of the Mass.

The Mass was the name that had been given to the Holy Communion, or the Lord's Supper. In Jerusalem on the night before he was crucified, Jesus had gathered his disciples around him in the upper room. He told them that this was the last time they would be together on this earth. He broke bread and gave it to them, and a cup of wine. The next day he would be crucified, and his lifeblood would be shed from his wounds on the cross. He said that whenever they should meet after he was gone, they were to remember his body given to the cross and his life laid down for them. When they took the bread and wine, it would be just as though they could see him in their midst again. He would be there, to make them strong in his love and in love for one another.

That was the blessed promise. The Church had not forgotten it, but it had let some of its meaning grow confused. Although the Mass was being celebrated in the name of Jesus, there was only a dim remembrance of what he was like and of what he would want Christian folk to be.

Since hardly any of the people could read, all they could do was listen to what the Church told them. So they went to Mass and heard the priest recite in Latin, and they watched him lift up the bread and wine. Then according to what they had been taught, there was an awful miracle. The bread became Christ's body, and he was sacrificed again for the sins of the world. If they were there at Mass, their own sins would be forgiven; and they could hope that they would go to heaven.

They did not know how that could be, but the Church said so, and who else was there to believe? Thus at any rate they were lifted out of despair. If they were obedient to the Church, they thought that they need not be afraid about the world to come.

Yet what happened from this faith was not all good. To be baptized and to go to Mass, as a Christian was obliged to do, was one thing; to live like a true Christian was something else, and more important. But the idea grew that the proper signs of being a Christian would take care of everything. So it came about that there were too many people in Europe whose so-called Christianity was hardly anything more than a name.

Another fact from which trouble was to come was the power the Church got because people were afraid. The less they knew, the more they imagined. They could not read the Gospels and learn about Jesus for themselves. Most of what they thought about him was that he would be the judge at the last day. Then he would reward the good, but sinners he would send to a hell that they were sure was full of devils waiting to torment them. Perhaps the Church could persuade him to have mercy. Perhaps the Virgin Mary, his mother, would plead with him. The Church said she would help everybody who turned to her if she was honored enough. And so there were prayers to the Virgin and prayers to the saints that they would ask Christ, the judge, not to be too hard. Only the Church could tell poor sinners how to get the Virgin and the saints to be on their side and to help them. Therefore nothing could be more fearful than not to be in good standing in the Church. Kings and governors could determine what would happen to a man in the few years of this life. But the pope and the bishops and the priests might determine what would happen to him through all the awful eternity to come.

Thus in what people believed about the Church was some of the darkness that belonged to the Dark Ages generally. And the Church itself of course was far from perfect. The goodness that comes from God was in it, but ignorance and the errors that all human beings make were in it too. Popes and bishops and the other clergy might be tempted to the same pride and selfishness they preached about. The more power the Church got, the more it might use that power for its own advantage. But all the same the Church was God's instrument for making the Dark Ages less dark than they would have been without it. The Church had its great examples of men who loved God and prayed and tried to do God's will. In a time of violence and confusion it prevented many cruelties. It gave help to the poor and the oppressed. It compelled powerful men, who might have been merciless because they feared no other power, to stop and remember God and the commandments of God by which they would be judged.

CHAPTER 16

NEW KINGDOMS RISE IN EUROPE

N THE great days of the power of Rome the paved Roman roads had stretched across all Europe. Travel had been safe. The Roman legions guarded the frontiers, and nobody feared invasion. Roman magistrates administered justice, and every Roman citizen could get his rights.

But all that was gone. There was no one power and no one law. Any bold and violent man was a law to himself. New kingdoms rose and fought one against another. The little people might be ground up in those struggles like grain between the millstones.

So there developed a new order of life. It was called feudalism. Every man and every class of men had a particular rank as related to the others. All the classes of people in a neighborhood were like separate layers of a pyramid, with each upper layer controlling the broader layers underneath it.

At the top was some masterful person who had got power because he or his fathers had fought to win it. He was the baron, and he and other barons made up the nobility. The baron owned the land. He might let some lesser nobleman occupy part of the lands that belonged to him, but that lesser lord not only had to pay rent to the baron; he had to promise also to fight under the baron's banner whenever there was any fighting to be done.

At the bottom were the common people. They had no land of their own and only the barest possessions of any kind. The lord might let his steward hand over to them little strips of ground to cultivate. Then they not only had to pay for part of the crops they raised; but on certain days of the week, no matter what happened to their own crops they had to go to work in the fields the lord had kept for himself. They lived in mean little hovels, plastered with mud and roofed with thatch. They had to take off their hats and bow whenever a nobleman rode by. But at least they were not as bad off as they might have been if they had had to shift entirely for themselves. The baron and his men-at-arms would protect them from outside enemies. And in the court which the baron held in the great hall of his stone castle they might get a rough justice if anyone had injured them.

At the top of the nobility was the king. All the barons had to swear fealty to the king, just as all those beneath the barons had to swear fealty to the barons. This was an oath of loyalty, which meant that each had to serve at the command of the one above. The common people for many centuries did not count for much. Whoever wanted backing would need to have the favor of the barons or the king.

In 754, nearly three hundred years after the beginning of what history has called the Dark Ages, Pope Stephen II found himself in danger. The barbarian Lombards who had settled in the north of Italy were constantly threatening Rome. Pope Stephen made a journey into France to ask for help. There he found that the army had taken its commander and made him king in place of the former king, who had been deposed and had gone into a monastery. The new king's name was Pepin, who came to be known as Pepin the Short. But whether he was short or not, he was the kind of ally the pope was looking for. He was the son of the great Charles Martel, Charles the Hammer, who had saved Europe from the Mohammedan invaders by his victory at Tours. Although Pepin was king already, the pope crowned him in the name of the Church. And he appealed to Pepin to bring his army down to Italy and teach the Lombards to behave.

So Pepin came. He marched into the Lombards' country as a conqueror. The Lombards were to let the pope alone, and they were to be punished for what they had done to him already. They should surrender five of their cities, including the ancient city of Ravenna—the city from which the last official of the emperor in Constantinople had been driven out three hundred years before. These five cities, and the country round them, Pepin gave to the pope to belong to him.

That was the beginning of something that was to make an immense difference in history for all the hundreds of years to follow. For when the pope thus had lands and cities over which he himself was the only ruler, he was no longer just a bishop of the Church. His business had been to be a shepherd of the souls of men in the name of Jesus Christ. But now he was to become more and more like one of the great barons, who controlled large territories, and ordered everything that people did, and collected taxes, and grew rich. The time was soon to come when popes would seem more concerned to get more land and more power than they would be concerned to remember the words of Jesus that "whosoever of you will be the chiefest, shall be servant of all."

Not long afterward another pope was to have important dealing with another king. Pepin's son, who succeeded him, was Charles—called Charles the Great or, as it was in French, Charlemagne.

Charlemagne was brought up a Christian, and he meant to be one. He could read, which in those days not even all kings could do. The book he read most of all was Augustine's *City of God,* which told that the Church would endure when kingdoms and empires perished. Charlemagne had at his court the great scholar Alcuin, and he liked to converse with Alcuin and with other learned men. He set up schools in his kingdom, particularly in order that the clergy should get some education; and he tried to see to it that all should worship and behave themselves in the way the Church had taught.

But there were other sides also to his idea of being a Christian. For twenty-five years, off and on, he was fighting the Saxon tribes in the north. He wanted to convert them to Christianity too, and he had his own way of doing it—a way that was very different from the forgotten words of Jesus that he had come "not to destroy men's lives but to save them." Charlemagne killed the Saxons without mercy as long as they were fighting; and when they surrendered, he gave the rest of them the choice between being killed or being baptized. And when they preferred not being killed, he sent for priests and had the Saxons baptized by the hundreds. So those who were left of whole tribes were thus made

Christian in name, though of course they had hardly any idea of the meaning of it all.

Meanwhile at Rome, Pope Leo III was in trouble and needed help wherever he could get it. A savage gang had set upon him in the streets of the city, beaten him, and left him battered and half blind. As soon as he could, Leo went off to France to appeal to Charlemagne, as Pope Stephen had appealed to Charlemagne's father, Pepin.

Charlemagne came down to Rome to see what was the matter there and to stop the violence against the pope.

Meanwhile a new idea was working in Leo's mind. The emperor in Constantinople was far away and seemed of no use to anybody in the West. There needed to be someone big enough to have the authority that the Roman emperor used to have, and strong enough to keep the peace. Why not Charlemagne? If the pope should crown him in the name of the Church, then the people would feel that it was the Church who had chosen Charlemagne and made him emperor. And Charlemagne would have to be the grateful protector of the Church.

So there came a day in the year 800 when Charlemagne went into St. Peter's Church to say his prayers. While he was kneeling there, the pope came silently up behind him. Before Charlemagne knew what was happening, the pope placed a crown on his head. A crowd of people, instructed perhaps beforehand by the pope, shouted out their honor to "Charles, most pious and august, crowned by God, the great and peace-bringing emperor!"

Charlemagne himself was not so pleased. He would rather have arranged his own crowning than have the pope do it. He did not want it to appear that it was the pope who had given him authority when as a matter of fact it was he who had been protecting the pope. He may have foreseen that a time might come—as indeed it did—when popes would claim that emperors, like everybody else, must be servants of the Church.

But however that might be, Charlemagne had been crowned as the first head of what was called the Holy Roman Empire. That was meant to be a rulership over many countries, held together as most of the world once had been held together by the empire of Rome. But there was one difference. This was to be the *Holy* Roman Empire. It was to be side by side with the Christian Church. It was supposed to govern according to the commandments of Christ.

This Holy Roman Empire was to exist for more than a thousand years. Sometimes its emperor had much power, especially in Germany and France. Sometimes he had very little. The great question was as to who would really come nearer to being the ruler of Europe, the emperor or the pope.

CHAPTER 17

CHIVALRY AND THE CRUSADES

ROUND THE year 1000 the Dark Ages were coming to an end and what were to be called the Middle or the Medieval Ages beginning. That does not mean, of course, that there was a sharp line on the other side of which everything was better. The change was gradual. But it was real. It was like the slow passing of a shadow and the coming in of a new day.

The schools that Charlemagne had started had made a difference. One of the great scholars whom Charlemagne had brought to his court used to cry out to the people who gathered round him, "Ho, everyone that desires wisdom, let him draw near and take it at our hands; for it is wisdom that we have for sale."

At first the schools were mostly connected with some church or monastery. But before long there began to grow up real universities, for the study of the law of the Church and theology and medicine. One of the earliest and greatest of these was the University of Paris, which began shortly after the year 1100. Others were in Italy and a little later at Oxford and Cambridge in England. At the start there were no great buildings. Young men lived in the town as best they could and came to the teacher wherever he could get a place for them to sit and listen. But the lack of buildings did not matter when men were hungry to get knowledge.

Now that men were learning more and really beginning to think, there was a stirring of new life in the Church and everywhere else.

Also something else was happening that would prove to be very important in another way. This was the beginning of what was called the age of chivalry.

The great barons, as we have seen, owned the land. The common people were servants in the lord's castle and peasants who plowed his fields. What were the sons of the nobility to do? They had no idea of working with their hands. A few went into monasteries. Some became bishops and grew to be as powerful as any baron. But what most of them were mainly interested in was fighting. There could be plenty of that, for Europe had not settled down to any general law and order. Each baron or other great lord ruled his own domain; and all his retainers—which meant all men subject to him—had to come to his banner when he called. And, any time, fighting might break out between the lord of some castle and another one with whom he had a quarrel.

Since this was so, it was necessary that there should be training. A nobleman would have young men who waited on him and would get him ready for battle. These were his squires. The time might come when a squire would be ready himself to become a champion. In those days there were no such things as gunpowder and rifles and cannon. Men fought hand to hand with lances, swords, and daggers. And they fought in armor. Blacksmiths hammered out iron on their anvils; and from the iron plates the expert armorers made the jointed armor that was to cover the legs, the arms, and the body, and a crested helmet with a visor that would protect the face. A man had to learn to wear his armor, to manage his horse, and to use his weapons. Then if he was judged to be worthy, he could be made a knight.

"Knight" and "knightly" are words that still have a noble sound. To say that someone is a knightly man would mean that he is brave and true and generous. That is what the knights in Europe in the days when they rode abroad and fought were supposed to be. Before the day when he was to be made a knight, a man kept his all-night vigil. This meant that, having bathed and clothed himself in white, he knelt alone all night before the church's altar to say his prayers that he might be a faithful knight. Then in a ceremony where other knights were gathered, his spurs were put on him and he was given the accolade, the touch of a sword across his shoulder. Thus he was admitted to the order of knighthood, having sworn to the code of honor by which all knights were bound. He pledged himself never to do outrageousity, nor murder, and always to flee treason. Also, by no mean to be cruel, but to give mercy unto him that asketh mercy . . . , and always to do ladies, damsels, and gentlewomen succour upon pain of death. Also, that no man take no battles in a wrongful quarrel for no law, nor for no world's goods.

But there were two sides to knighthood and two sides to the way the Church thought about it. On the one hand, glorious traditions grew up about the knights, such as in early England, the stories of King Arthur and his knights of Camelot, such as Lancelot and Galahad. And the same was true of Roland, the hero of France. It was supposed that the knights went out to challenge the castles of evil men and to rescue maidens in distress. And the ceremony when a man was made a knight was often given a religious meaning. He was supposed to be a servant of God as well as to win honor of men.

On the other hand, most of the time the knights were not doing anything useful. They fought against one another in tournaments, where the only point was to see who could prove himself to have the most deadly strength and skill. While the nobility and their ladies looked on, two knights would enter what were called the lists. Fully armored and on horseback, they would take their positions at opposite ends of the tournament field. Then with their lances lowered they would spur their horses and come thundering toward each other. If the lance of one knight struck the other knight squarely, that knight might be hurled from his saddle; and the first knight, leaping from his horse and drawing his sword, would demand his rival's surrender. In those encounters men might be maimed and sometimes killed.

Also in other ways there was much cruelty. When there was a battle, the knights of the victorious side might treat the knights among their enemies with great regard and courtesy; but there was no concern for the common people. If a castle or a town was taken, the ordinary crowd might be slaughtered without mercy. And a knight who met a peasant on the road or passed the hovel where he lived might treat him and all his family as the scum of the earth.

Then to one of the popes there came a new idea. Why not start the knights at something that would bring glory to the Church?

For more than four hundred years the land of Palestine had been in the hands of the Mohammedans. Christian pilgrims would try to go to Jerusalem to worship in the city where Christ had been crucified. Sometimes they would be mistreated. And, anyway, it seemed a bitter thing that those whom the Christians called infidels should have possession of the sacred places. Pope Urban II reflected upon that. Why not rouse all Christian nations to go and win back the Holy Land?

So in 1095 the pope went into France. A great council of the Church was held in the city of Clermont. Princes and bishops were there, and knights by the thousand and a huge multitude of the people. The pope spoke to the crowd that packed the great central square of the city.

"Christian warriors," he exclaimed, "you seek without end for vain pretexts for war. Rejoice, for today you have found true ones! Go and fight against the infidels. Go and fight for the deliverance of the holy places. If you triumph, the kingdoms of the East will be yours. If you are conquered, you will have the glory of dying in the very same place as Jesus Christ; and God will not forget that he shall have found you in his holy ranks."

It was just as though fire had been dropped into dry fuel. Here was the pope, who was thought of as the head of the Church, telling them that it was their religious duty to go and win back the Holy Land. And that in doing it they would save their souls.

Here would be a crusade—a war in the name of Christ under the banner of the cross. The shout went up *"Deus vult"*—"God wills it!"

From Clermont the great excitement swept through France and across all Europe. Not only the nobility began to answer. So did crowds of the common people.

It was a religious excitement, and it was also something else. Europe had been in a bad way. In many parts of it there had been the dreadful sickness called the plague. Also there had been poor harvests and little food. Many people had been hungry. Now the Church at the Council of Clermont had said that all those who went on the crusade would be freed from taxes, and no debts they owed could be collected. And if they should get to the Mohammedan countries, perhaps they who owned nothing at home could seize new lands and possessions.

Peter the Hermit, a monk who had been to Jerusalem, went about preaching in all the towns. The pope had not meant the crusade to begin until the real fighting men were ready. But the common people took what crude weapons they had, pikes and pitchforks and clubs, and followed their own leaders. They filled the roads going east. In their ignorance they had no idea just where they were to go or how far it was. They would come to a castle or to a town, and they would ask, "Is this Jerusalem?" They did not know that it was hundreds and hundreds of miles away, and that most of them would die without ever coming near it.

Meanwhile the knights were arming. By August, 1096, they were ready. On their horses, followed by their servants and retainers, they set out in their glittering array. They rode as far as Constantinople. There they halted and made agreement with the Eastern emperor. Then they crossed into Asia Minor. They captured the city of Nicaea. Forcing their slow way ahead, they captured Tarsus, where the apostle Paul was born. Then they took the great city of Antioch. And at last on one thrilling day the crusaders came within sight of Jerusalem.

They laid siege to the city and broke through its walls. That was in 1099. It had been three years since the trampling of their horses first raised dust clouds on the long roads that led from Europe. Now their banners were planted where they had sworn to bring them.

But this was not the end. It was only the beginning. Under Godfrey of Bouillon they established the kingdom of Jerusalem. But holding it and defending it was another matter. For two hundred years new armies had to keep coming from Europe to bring help against the Moslems, who would never stay defeated. Sometimes these armies were led by kings, such as Richard I of England, called the Lionhearted, and Louis IX, called St. Louis, of France. Once the wild excitement spread even to the children, in what came to be called the Children's Crusade. Thousands of

them flocked together without weapons and without any provisions except what they could beg along the way. They thought that somehow they would get to the Holy Land and that a miracle would give them victory. But many of them perished on the roads. And some who got down into Italy and thought that they would find ships to carry them by sea fell into the hands of pirates and were sold as slaves.

In the end not even all the crusading armies and all the knights and kings could succeed. They had what they meant to be a holy purpose, but there was much they did not understand. Their wars were often blind and cruel. They thought they could create a Christian kingdom by the sword. But that is not the way in which the world can ever be won for Christ.

CHAPTER 18

POPES AND EMPERORS

HROUGH THE long years when the roads of Europe shook with the hoofbeats of the crusaders riding toward the wars in Palestine, another and different sort of struggle went on in Europe itself. It was the struggle between the popes and the emperors.

The pope was the bishop of Rome, and at first he had been only that. He was chosen by the clergy and the people of Rome as their bishop just as other cities chose their bishops too. He might have no more authority over the whole Church than any other bishop had. But the popes had long since begun to declare that they did have more authority. It was claimed (though without any sure proof) that the church in Rome had been founded by the apostle Peter, that Peter was the chief of the apostles, and therefore that whoever was bishop of Rome must always be the chief among all bishops.

Moreover, there grew up the story that the Emperor Constantine had been healed of leprosy by the Roman Bishop Sylvester and that out of gratitude he had given to him and to the popes after him his palace in Rome and the "city of Rome and all the provinces, districts, and cities of Italy or of the Western regions." That was not a fact, but many people believed it. And many people believed also some writings that a monk named Isadore had put together, which he said showed that the bishops of Rome had always had the right to decide matters for the Church everywhere.

In the East, where emperors who had succeeded Constantine still ruled in Constantinople, the bishop of Rome was not much listened to. Under the protection of the Eastern emperor the patriarch of Constantinople was the chief figure. Differences between the Orthodox Church in the East and the church in the West had been increasing. In the Eastern church there had been a long struggle against allowing images of Christ, the Virgin Mary,

95

and the saints to stand in the churches. It was finally decided that these icons, as the Greeks called them, could be kept if they were flat pictures instead of round figures. But the Roman Church still encouraged the use of images. The Eastern church said in the Nicene Creed that the Holy Spirit comes from God the Father, not from both God the Father and Christ the Son, as the Roman Church declared. The Eastern clergy except the bishops could be married, but in the West it was beginning to be ruled that none could marry. Because of these and other disagreements, including one as to what is said about the Holy Spirit in the Nicene Creed, the Orthodox Church and the Church of Rome drifted further apart, until in 1054 they broke connections altogether.

Christianity had been carried from Constantinople into Russia, and among the Serbs and the Bulgars who had established their kingdoms in Eastern Europe. So all these peoples belonged to the Orthodox Church. But in the West the authority of the pope kept growing, and the bishops and priests in many countries looked to him as their head. Consequently it made a great difference who was pope and who chose him.

For many years after Charlemagne was crowned in the year 800 as the first emperor of the Holy Roman Empire, the emperors tried to dictate who the pope should be. When the emperor was powerful, he could do it. Henry III, king of Germany and also emperor, got rid of three rivals who claimed each one to have been elected pope. Then he chose the next pope and the next one after him. It looked as though the emperor would rule the Church.

But now began a different story. New forces were working in the Church. They were to change its life and give it presently a new kind of power.

In the first place there needed to be changes inside. Many bishops and other clergy who ought to have been examples of real religion were no better than anybody else. To be a bishop or to be the abbot of a monastery in those times meant to own large lands and to receive contributions which the poor peasants had to pay. So it happened that men who cared nothing for the things of God would get themselves made bishops because of the gain they could get out of that. Greed and corruption had spread through the Church.

A change came with a new pope. He was Leo IX, and one of the men who was closest to him was the monk Hildebrand. These and others in Rome were determined to purify the Church. The pope indignantly condemned those who had got their positions by bribery. He put the worst of the bishops out of office. He set up new standards of discipline for the clergy generally.

All decent men could be glad of that. But something else was done, about which there could be disagreement as to whether it was good or bad. Up to this time of the eleventh century bishops and other clergy of the Church could be married. Now the decree went out from Rome that none of them could be married any more. One reason for that was the belief that men who had no families to consider would be more obedient to the pope.

In 1070 Hildebrand was elected pope. He took the name of Gregory VII. Now for the next 150 years popes were to match their authority against the authority of kings and emperors. The struggle was to see who should control the life and affairs of the western world.

There were many matters in which there could be collision. Here were some of them:

Who should appoint the bishops and other great persons of the Church? Only the head of the Church, said the pope. But bishops might be powerful feudal lords, wealthy and important. The king or the emperor did not want to have in his country great figures who would swear faith to a pope and not to him. He must have his say as to who were appointed and as to what they were pledged to do.

What about the laws men were to be judged by and the courts where they must appear? The king of England or the king of France or the emperor of Germany wanted everybody to be subject alike to his own country's laws. But the pope insisted that all matters concerning the Church should be carried to Rome for judgment.

What about taxes and money? The pope claimed that heavy

contributions must come to Rome from every bishopric and from every church foundation anywhere. But what would happen to a country if money was thus being always drained out of it and very little coming back?

And when some question arose of right or wrong, or of what could be permitted or forbidden, who should have the last word? When ordinary people were concerned, it might be all very well for the Church to set up its laws. But suppose a king wanted to divorce his queen, and the pope forbade it. Or suppose a pope actually claimed the right to put some sovereign off his throne and to choose another to succeed him. Any king or emperor would be up in arms against any such idea as that.

And that was exactly the idea that Gregory VII had. Not only an idea; it was his proud and positive conviction. Soon after he had been made pope, he came into collision with Henry IV of Germany, mostly about who should or should not be made bishops. Henry had larger armies than the pope, but the pope had two weapons which in those days were more terrifying than any armies. They were the excommunication and the interdict.

Excommunication meant that a man was cut off from the Church. He was branded as a sinner condemned. He could not come to any service of the Church that might bring him God's forgiveness. If he died, he could not be buried in holy ground. He was counted as a lost soul. And the awful power of the Church's teaching made him believe it.

The interdict was even worse. It fell not only upon a single person but upon a whole country. If a king was excommunicated and his kingdom laid under an interdict, it meant that there could be no church services for anybody, no baptisms, no marriages, no saying of the Mass, no Christian burial. When people believed that the Church had power over their souls for this life and the life to come, the interdict could fall upon them like a black and stifling darkness.

The quarrel between Gregory VII and Henry IV of Germany grew more and more angry. Each one, pope and king, was determined to be obeyed. Henry sent to the pope an insulting letter, addressed to the "monk Hildebrand." He threatened to set up another pope in his place.

Then Gregory answered, and his answer to Henry was excommunication. "I bind him," he wrote, "with the chain of anathema," which meant the Church's curse in the name of God. And he did not stop with that. "I prohibit to Henry the king," he wrote, "the rule of the whole kingdom of Germany and Italy." He set all Christians free from any oaths of loyalty "they have sworn or shall swear to him, and I forbid anyone to serve him as king."

When Henry heard that he had been excommunicated, he tried at first to act as though nothing had happened. With his army and the princes of Germany back of him he thought he could defy the pope. But the princes began to be afraid of having anything to do with a man who was excommunicated from the Church. One by one they deserted Henry. Now it was his turn to be afraid. There was nothing left except for him to yield.

About Christmastime in the year 1076 Henry started from Germany to go to Italy and make his peace with the pope. His queen was with him and a handful of attendants. It was the dead of winter and bitter cold. On the great mountains of the Alps that he had to cross, the snow and ice were deep. Horses could not keep their feet and slipped and floundered. Men had to crawl sometimes on their hands and knees. Exhausted and half frozen, they arrived at length in Italy.

The pope had come north from Rome. Not sure yet of what Henry meant to do, he had shut himself up in the walled castle of Canossa. But Henry had no thought now of violence. He had come to get rid of the excommunication.

Dressed in a rough woolen shirt and with bare feet, Henry stood all day in the snow in the courtyard of the castle. He knocked at the door. But the door did not open.

Another day he stood there. But again no answer came to him from within the castle.

Only on the third day did the pope allow the door to open

and the king to come in. And Henry knelt down in tears before the pope, kissed his hands and begged forgiveness.

All over Europe, when the news was known, men held their breath to see the power of the pope. The greatest king in Europe had been obliged to kneel to him.

Gregory had triumphed. Now, however, he tried to carry his triumph too far. He still refused to crown Henry as emperor of the Holy Roman Empire. He helped some of the princes of Germany to try to elect another king. He excommunicated Henry a second time. But this time neither Henry nor the princes in Germany were frightened, but only angered. Henry marched with an army against Rome. Rome was captured and another pope set up. Gregory fled to the city of Salerno, and there he died in exile.

All the same his effect on history was not ended. It had only begun. He had made plain the vast claim of the popes to be the supreme rulers of their world. He had done that in what he demanded not only of the king of Germany but of kings in France and Hungary and Spain and Denmark and even England. He declared that Christ himself through Peter had given all authority to the Church of Rome, and that to that church "he has subjected the principalities, powers and everything else which is sublime upon earth."

That was what Gregory believed, even though it was not a fact. The popes who followed him chose to believe it also. And not only that. For the next two hundred years and more they made most of the western world believe it.

So it happened that Pope Urban II eleven years after the death of Gregory dared to consider that he had authority enough to launch the crusades. And tens of thousands of men, as we have seen, listened to him and answered him, and left their homes to march on the long and perilous way to win back the Holy Land.

So it happened also that a king as proud and powerful as Henry II of England had to humble himself before a rebuke from Rome. Thomas Becket, the archbishop of Canterbury, had roused the anger of the king by keeping some of the clergy from being tried in the king's courts. One day in 1171 in a burst of temper the king cried out, "Will no one rid me of this pestilent priest?" Three knights who heard him went off without the king's knowing it and killed the archbishop before the altar of his own church. A wave of horror went through England. People began to think of Becket as a sort of saint, and the spot where he was slain became a shrine to which thousands came on pilgrimage. And at the demand of Pope Alexander III, Henry himself had to come there and kneel and do penance—which meant to confess his part in the crime against the representative of the pope.

But the high point of the power of the popes was still to come. From 1198 to 1216 the pope was Innocent III. He believed completely in what Gregory had claimed more than a hundred years before—that the pope was meant to be the ruler above all rulers. He forced Philip of France to take back his queen whom he had tried to divorce. He compelled the emperor of Germany to acknowledge his authority. And when King John of England resisted him, Innocent brought the king to such a surrender as could hardly have been believed. John handed over his kingdom as though it belonged to the pope, and he was to rule only as the pope's servant. And every year he would send a great sum of money to Rome.

Thus it seemed that the popes had risen to the height of earthly power. And so they had. But it was a dangerous sort of power that was to bring evil results. The words of Jesus had been forgotten when he said to Pilate, "My kingdom is not of this world." The popes had been trying to build a kingdom for the Church in proud ambition and sometimes by craft and by force. But the kingdom of the spirit cannot be built that way.

CHAPTER 19

A SAINT WHO
MADE MEN REMEMBER CHRIST

HILE THE popes were building up their authority and supposing that thus they were making the Church great, other quieter things were happening that were much nearer to the spirit of Christ.

In 1182 in the Italian town of Assisi there was born a boy baptized as Giovanni Bernardone, nicknamed Francesco, and after his short life to be known forever as St. Francis. His father was a rich merchant, who wanted his son to be such a person as he was. He gave him fine clothes and money to spend. And Francis enjoyed it all. He was the leader of the reckless young men who had nothing to do except to amuse themselves. He was so gay and laughing that he could make friends with everybody. He liked adventure, and he fought for Assisi in a battle with Perugia, the city perched on a great hill nearby. He loved to sing; and he loved the beautiful country round about, with its deep-blue Italian sky, its trees where the birds sang, and its green valley where the olives grew. To be carefree and charming—that seemed to be enough for him.

But all the while deep down he was not satisfied. He wanted something that he could give his heart to: something different from the life he knew.

One day he had given a banquet to a group of his friends, and afterward they all went out singing through the streets. Later on the others missed him. When they found Francis again, he was like a man in a trance. Something had happened to him that astonished them and was too big for him to explain.

Days passed by, while Francis went out often into the hills to think and to be alone. Then he set off on a pilgrimage to Rome. There he saw a crowd of beggars; and almost before he

102

knew it, he had stripped off the clothes he wore as the rich merchant's son, given them to one of the beggars, and put on the beggar's rags.

And that was not all. When he had come back home and to the wealth and ease of his father's house, he was out riding one day on his horse. Near Assisi there was a sort of hospital where people who had leprosy were herded together. Leprosy was the most dreadful of all diseases, and Francis had a horror of it. But on the road this day he met a leper. Francis reined back his horse so violently that the horse almost threw him. Then with a great rush of pity Francis dismounted, took the leper in his arms, and kissed his dreadful-looking face.

From that moment Francis' whole life was changed. He began to go among the lepers and to nurse them. People began to think he was out of his mind. They were afraid, too, that he might get leprosy and spread it. They threw sticks and mud at him as he went by.

There was a little old chapel outside of Assisi, almost ready to fall down, where one poor priest lived. Francis used to go there to pray. One day the thought came to him, as though a voice had spoken, that he must help to build the old chapel up again. So he took some of the money his father would have given him for himself and bought stone to build with.

But by now his father was furious. What son of his was this who was making all the people of Assisi point their fingers at him as though he were a lunatic—going among lepers, having mud thrown at him in the streets, wasting money on a tumbledown church! He would not stand it.

So Pietro Bernardone, the rich merchant, took Francis before the bishop. He said he wanted everybody to understand that none of his money should belong to a son like that. He did not deserve to have even the clothes he had on.

Then an astonishing thing happened. Francis rose and spoke to the bishop.

"My lord," he said, "I not only will have no more of my father's money; I will give back to him all I can of what he has given me."

Then he went out of the bishop's hall. When he came back, the people gasped. There he was, stark naked, except for a cloth around his waist. He laid his clothes down at his father's feet.

"Listen, all of you," he said. "I return to Pietro Bernardone, who has been my father, all that he has given to me. Now I turn only to 'our Father, who art in heaven.' "

The bishop had someone go and find an old, worn cloak. He put it round Francis, and Francis took a piece of chalk and marked a cross upon it. Then he went out alone.

It was to turn out that this day when he had seemed to give up everything he had gained everything. He could remember the words of Jesus "Whoever loses his life for my sake and the gospel's shall save it."

For three years it might have looked as though Francis was doing nothing that mattered much. He set himself to rebuild the poor little St. Damian's Chapel and also another half-ruined old church, called St. Mary of the Angels. He begged stone from those who might give it to him, and he did the work with his own hands.

One day at St. Damian's, as he listened to the reading of the gospel, these were the words of Jesus that he heard: *"Preach as you go, saying, 'The kingdom of heaven is at hand.' Heal the sick, raise the dead, cleanse lepers, cast out demons. You received without pay, give without pay. Take no gold, nor silver, nor copper in your belts, no bag for your journey, . . . for the laborer deserves his food."*

Over the altar of the old chapel there was a rude carving of Jesus on the cross. Francis looked at it, and his heart was full. "For the love of him," he said to himself, "I will go out and do what he told his disciples."

So in a robe of rough brown cloth such as the poorest peasants wore at work, with a piece of rope tied round his waist, Francis began to preach in the streets of Assisi. When he had first laid down his clothes in the bishop's palace and had left his father's house, people thought he must be crazy. But there was something about him now that made them stop and listen. He preached to them that this is God's world and that they were his children, that Jesus had lived and died to bring them the love of God, and that they should learn to be kind to one another. They might have thought they had heard all that before, but now it was different. The words were like a torch that now for the first time burst into flame. Francis had made the gospel real. They had seen him visiting the lepers. They had watched him carrying stone to build the churches, singing as he used to do when he was the gay young blade, but singing now in pure joy for the love of God. They saw that this Francis who had been rich had made himself a brother to all the sick and the poor. He made them think of Jesus, because like Jesus "he went about doing good."

Two important men in Assisi heard him preach, and their hearts were moved. One was Bernard of Quintavalle, a nobleman. He asked Francis to his house. He told Francis that he would surrender everything he had to follow Christ. And he said that his friend, Dr. Peter Cathanii, a great lawyer, was ready to do the same.

So the three of them went to church together and prayed. Then they opened the Gospels to see what might be written there. This is what they read:

"If any man will come after me, let him deny himself, and take up his cross, and follow me."

"If thou wilt be perfect, go and sell that thou hast, and give to the poor."

"And he commanded them that they should take nothing for their journey."

"Brothers," said Francis, "this shall be the rule for us and for any others who may come with us." They should be sworn to poverty and to obedience to nothing but the service of Christ.

Soon after that, to the amazement of all Assisi, Bernard of Quintavalle stood in the central square and gave away his possessions to the poor. Then he and Peter Cathanii and Francis went to live in a little hut they built by the church of St. Mary of the Angels.

Thus with two or three began the fellowship that was to grow quickly into thousands. They called themselves the "little brothers of the poor." They were to wear the brown frock of the peasants, to have no money of their own, to live only by such work as they could do from day to day or by food that people gave them. The monks lived in their monasteries, mostly apart from other people. But the followers of Francis were to have no fixed home of their own. They were to go everywhere, in the streets of towns or amongst the country folk, telling all they met of Christ.

When the number of his companions had grown to twelve, Francis decided he must ask the blessing of the Church. Therefore he journeyed to Rome to appear before the pope.

Two men more unlike could hardly have been imagined. The pope was the great Innocent III. There he sat, the person who at that moment was the most powerful in the whole western world, in the splendor of the papal palace. And there before him, barefoot, stood the man who had nothing of his own except the dusty brown robe he wore and the rope that held it together round his waist.

The great pope pondered. Was this some crazy enthusiasm that the Church should have nothing to do with? Or was it a work of God?

Innocent was wise enough to believe that here might be a power better than the power he had wielded over emperors and kings. He gave his blessing to Francis, and Francis went back to Assisi.

From that time his followers—afterward to be called the Franciscan Order—increased by leaps and bounds. They spread through all countries, carrying the gospel to the common people, living in poverty as they had seen Francis do. As for Francis himself he journeyed preaching not only in Italy but as far away as Spain and Egypt and Palestine. Nobody had ever seen anyone quite like him. He was so joyous that people called him God's minstrel, for he seemed to make the gospel as beautiful and exciting as a song. Because he trusted God completely, there was nothing of which he was afraid. Because of his love and gentleness people flocked about him, and even the wild creatures of God's earth somehow understood that he was different. Birds

would light on his shoulders and on his hand; and there was a story that once he talked to a hungry wolf, and the wolf grew tame.

So while Francis lived and his spirit prevailed, the Franciscan Order—or the Friars—were like a new goodness spread through all the common life of Europe. And Francis himself grew more and more the saint that men were afterward to call him. Though his strength failed and he wore his body out in his tireless service, he never ceased rejoicing in the glory of all God's creation and the wonderfulness of life. He wrote a "Canticle of the Sun," in praise of sun and moon and stars, and of all the familiar blessings of the earth. He could praise God no less for pain and suffering, and he meditated so much on Christ that at the end of his life there had come upon his hands and feet black marks like the nails that held Christ to the cross. And as he was dying, he called Brother Angelo and Brother Leo to him, and bade them sing the "Canticle of the Sun." Then flinging up his hands, he cried, "Welcome, Sister Death! Praise ye and bless ye the Lord; give thanks unto him and serve him with all humility."

CHAPTER 20

RELIGION IN THE MIDDLE AGES

HILE THE popes were struggling with the emperors for world power for the Church, the ordinary people were more concerned with what went on where they lived. They listened to the preaching of the friars. They came to church to hear the Mass, made confession of their sins, and wanted to be buried at last in holy ground.

Great scenes and truths from the Bible were put into the mystery plays and morality plays that were written and performed all through the Middle Ages, sometimes outdoors, more often in the church. Some of the earliest ones were in Latin, like the Mass, so that the people could gather their meaning only by watching the action as that went on. But more and more, especially in England, they were written in language that everybody understood. Often the broad humor of the crowd was reflected in them, as in the quarrel between Noah and his wife in *Noah's Flood* when Noah beat his wife to make her move faster into the ark. Or as in the devils that came out from the crude scenery that represented the mouth of hell. But beauty and pathos were in them too, as when Isaac, about to be sacrificed by Abraham, said piteously to his father:

> Now I wold to God my moder were here on this hyll
> Sche wold knele for me on both hyr kneys
> To save my lyffe.

One after another events and characters from both the Old Testament and the New would be brought to mind. There were plays about Adam and Eve, about Isaac and Rebecca and Jacob and Esau, about Balaam and some of the prophets, about the Virgin Mary and the Angel Gabriel and the shepherds in the fields of Bethlehem and the birth of Jesus, about the Resurrection, about the conversion of the apostle Paul.

Or it might be that one of these dramas that the people flocked to see did not deal with particular Bible scenes but with the whole solemn and fearful message which the Bible seemed to them to bring. Such was the morality play of *Everyman*. It begins with the voice of God summoning Death to go for Everyman. Young and gay and careless, Everyman comes to his shocked encounter with the waiting Death, who points him to the grave into which he must go down. Everyman begs for companions who may help him—his friends, his kindred, his possessions—but none of these can avail him now. And neither can he take with him any of the aspects of himself which had been his satisfaction: not his beauty, nor his strength, nor his smartness, nor any of the five senses of his body. Then Knowledge (the knowledge that the church of the Middle Ages sought to have all men accept) leads him to confession and to the Mass; and after that one companion will go with him and bring to God a plea for him at last. This companion is Good Deeds. In the strength of the plea that Good Deeds makes, Everyman descends into his grave and prays to be delivered

> from the fiend's boast
> And to appear with that blessed host
> That shall be saved at the Day of Doom.

Nobody can ever know the names of all the little people who were trying to be Christians as well as they knew how. But everyone can see some of the results of their religion. Those results are the great church buildings and cathedrals that after hundreds of years still stand not only in cities but in small towns of France, and England, and Germany, and Spain.

From about a century before Francis of Assisi was born to two hundred or more years after that was the great age of building. Much of it began with the monks. Money came to the monasteries from rich lords who wanted the prayers of the monks for their sins when they were living and for their souls when they died. So the monks built vast and beautiful churches that towered over a whole countryside. Or there might be wanted a new church that should belong especially to a bishop, which is the meaning of a cathedral. One bishop might want his cathedral to be larger and more magnificent than any other that had been built, and he would have immense plans drawn.

But the people did the building. That was the wonderful thing. It was not just a matter of hiring a few special workmen, while all the rest looked on or went about their separate business. Everybody could have a hand in what was being done. If they were not among the expert masons or the sculptors or the glassmakers, they could help haul the materials. And they did. Hundreds of men and women would take hold of the ropes to drag the carts that bore the heaviest blocks of stone. The children had their little carts. As the walls of the cathedrals rose, it was the whole town that was making its gift to God.

The houses in which the people lived were poor things made of wood, small and huddled together. The cathedral soared above them as the reminder of a world more glorious than the world their bodies lived in. When they went inside, the sounds of the noisy town were lost in its vast stillness. They could look up through the lofty arches to the dim, vaulted roof that seemed almost as high as heaven. And from the stained-glass windows the light fell in red and blue and gold and purple patterns on the floor.

Most of the people could not read. But in the cathedral that belonged to them and that their hands had built they could go and look at the long story of the religion they had been taught. On its outside walls and clustered about its doors were the carved figures of the Old Testament such as Abraham and Moses, the twelve apostles of the New Testament, the four evangelists who wrote the Gospels, kings and queens and saints in the long history of the Church. In the stained-glass windows they could see endlessly much more: Adam and Eve in the Garden of Eden, the angel with the flaming sword, the sacrifice of Isaac, Jacob's vision of the ladder to heaven, Moses coming with the Ten Commandments, Saul and Jonathan and David, and the prophets. And then they could turn to the windows that showed the little Child in the manger at Bethlehem and the shepherds and the Wise Men, and Jesus as a boy in the Temple, and Jesus teaching and healing and standing before Pilate and nailed on the cross to die, and rising from the dead, and coming again to his disciples before he went beyond their mortal sight.

The services in the cathedral were in Latin, and much that went on in them was a mystery to simple people. But to be there made them remember God. Here were the tombs and memorials of the dead, and the whole cathedral was a sign of the living faith that bound all souls together. Over the great central door might be the sculptured figure of Christ and the scene of the last judgment. Men and women looking at it might ask themselves on which side, the right or left, they would stand on that judgment day. But always from among the crooked streets or from the open country they could see the mighty shape of the cathedral with its spires and towers lifted to the sky, until it appeared to them "as a great ship in which man might sail to heaven."

CHAPTER 21

MEN WHO DARED TO THINK

OMETHING ELSE also was happening, which in time would tame the power of the popes and give a new meaning to the Church. People were beginning to think for themselves.

The growth of the universities in Paris and in other cities of Europe was spreading knowledge. The thousands who had gone to other lands on the crusades had come back with new ideas. When the crusades failed, many were restless and discontented. They began to have bitter questions about the Church under the rule of the popes. Some of their ideas went off in wild directions. But some were of a kind that gave new meaning to Christian life and thought.

When Innocent III was pope, there were people in the south of France called the Albigenses, because most of them at first had been in and around the city of Albi. They had begun to believe and to preach that the world had grown so evil that people ought to stop marrying and having children. They said the Church was worst of all—that the bishops were greedy and the priests wicked and lazy. They would follow their own beliefs and not come to the Church to hear what any priests or bishops had to say.

Their heresies seemed to Innocent to be deadly sin. The Albigenses had to be corrected.

Besides the Franciscans there had grown up a new order of preaching friars, called the Dominicans. They were the followers of Dominic, a Spaniard, who lived at the same time as Francis. The Franciscans were known above all for their vow of poverty and for the way they worked among the poor and among all simple folk. The Dominicans were more interested in being men of learning, so that they could teach the proper faith.

One of the Dominicans was the great scholar Thomas Aquinas, whose vast book the *Summa Theologiae* has been held for seven

113

hundred years in the Roman Catholic Church as the supreme summing up of its beliefs. Pope Innocent sent Dominic and his preaching followers to try to convert the Albigenses. Dominic did his best but without much success. At last he said, "I have exhorted you in vain, with gentleness, preaching, praying, and weeping. Now we shall rouse against you princes and prelates, and thus blows will avail where blessings and gentleness have been powerless."

In place of persuasion there was to be persecution. Pope Innocent genuinely believed that heresy, which was denying what the Church believed and taught, had to be stamped out. Better that people should suffer in their bodies than lose their souls. So he let loose the princes and barons of northern France to carry war into the south. In the name of religion there was invasion—and plundering and the burning of towns and torture and killing. Thousands of the Albigenses were ferociously put to death.

This was the beginning in Christian Europe of what became known by the dread name of the Inquisition. Agents of the Church arrested people suspected of any heresy and examined them. If they dared profess beliefs different from the Church's teaching, they were tortured with thumbscrews or their bodies twisted on the rack or condemned to be tied to the stake and burned alive. All this was done in grim good conscience. The rulers of the Church believed that no cruelty could be as bad as allowing the spread of heresy. To punish men here on earth was indeed a mercy, said the Inquisitors, if it could save men from denying the Church's faith and so from being punished afterward in hell.

Another and nobler group than the Albigenses were hunted by the Inquisition. They were Christians whom the Church ought to have been wise enough to welcome, as Pope Innocent had given his blessing to the followers of Francis. These were the Waldensians.

About the year 1170 in the city of Lyons in France a rich merchant named Peter Waldo sold his possessions and gave them to the poor. That was twelve years before Francis of Assisi was born. Peter Waldo declared also that the popes and bishops had let the Church grow corrupt and careless, until many of the people were like sheep without a shepherd. He said too that a man did not need the authority of the Church to preach the gospel. It depended on the Holy Spirit in his own heart. And if a man's heart was not right, no matter if he was priest or pope, he was no real minister of Christ.

From the beginning of the thirteenth century on, the Inquisition tried to destroy the Waldensians. It killed many and drove others into hiding. But in the little valleys of the Alps, Waldensian congregations survived, and still are there.

After Peter Waldo other men began to speak out as boldly as he had spoken. And they had more reason all the time. For as people looked at the popes in Rome, they respected them less and less. The successors of the great Pope Innocent were bent on keeping the power that he had had over emperors and kings. But they failed in that, and meanwhile they were failing in what was more important. Less than a hundred years after Innocent was dead, the popes became not much more than prisoners of the kings of France. Pope Boniface VIII, who had made proud claims of complete authority, was arrested by an armed force sent by the French king. When he died, the next pope was compelled to leave Rome and come to live in Avignon in the south of France. The cardinals—who are the ecclesiastics in the Church of Rome next in authority to the pope himself, and by whom the new pope is elected when the old pope dies—went with him.

There in Avignon for seventy years the popes had to stay, whether they wanted to or not. That time in history became known as the Babylonian Captivity, because the popes had lost their freedom as the people of Israel had lost theirs when they were carried captives into Babylon.

But the fact that the popes no longer had the worldly power that Gregory VII and Innocent III had had was not the worst of the matter. The trouble was that people began to feel that the Church was no better off wherever the popes might or might not be. The popes and all the cardinals who were in

Avignon with them seemed more interested in collecting contributions and keeping comfortable than they were in what might be happening to people's souls. All through the Church there were more laziness and greed than love of Christ and preaching of the gospel.

In England, John Wycliffe, who was born not long after the pope went to Avignon, gave voice to what honest men were thinking. He was a learned scholar of Oxford University and a priest of the Church. But he had a true concern for the common people. "Christians should stand to the death," he said, "for maintaining Christ's gospel and true understanding of it, gotten by holy life and great study, and not set their faith and trust in sinful prelates and their clerks."

That is exactly what the prelates (the ruling clergy of the Church) were, he said: sinful and not devoted either to great study or to a holy life. Instead of that they were worse than people who had never taken any vows of holiness. "They love worldly riches," said Wycliffe, "and labor for them night and day, in thought and deed; and labor little for God's worship and the saving of Christian souls." He accused the bishops of living in idle luxury and riding abroad in silks and furs while the poor people went in rags. The monks, he said, were fat and indolent; and the friars, instead of following the example of Francis of Assisi, would rather beg or steal than work, and were drunken and gluttonous besides.

Peter Waldo had said that a genuine Christian man did not have to wait for authority from the Church to go out and tell of Christ. John Wycliffe said the same. And in order that the common folk might actually be told of Christ, he had the Bible translated from Latin for the first time into the English tongue; and he sent out preachers to teach it directly to the people. He dared to say also that there was no such thing as a changing of the bread and wine by the priest at Mass into the body and blood of Christ—which the Church had taught that people *had* to believe if their souls were to be saved. They could be saved by believing the Bible and trying to live by it. And that would be true, Wycliffe declared, if the pope and all the priests were cast into hell, where he thought that some of them belonged.

Richard II, king of England, married Anne, a princess of Bohemia. Because of that the teachings of Wycliffe spread into the center of Europe. What he had said about evils in the Church was truer now than ever. The popes had come back from Avignon, but only to have things grow worse instead of better. Quarreling broke out among the cardinals. There were popes and rival popes, and some of them were men whose lives were scandalous.

Already in Bohemia there was stirring a spirit of protest against some of the beliefs and practices of the Church. Men there, as in England, were beginning to denounce corruption among the clergy and to look back to the Bible for a rule of life.

At the University of Prague first as a student and then as a distinguished member of its faculty was John Huss. When the writings of Wycliffe came into Bohemia, Huss was much impressed by them and began to use them in his teaching. He was not only a man of wide learning. He was a preacher of great conviction and power. Crowds flocked to hear him. When he denounced the evils in the Church, he was telling what everybody knew and what most people wanted to be rid of. But the more these ordinary people made Huss their hero, the more the men high up in the Church began to fear him. He had gone too far, they said. He was like Wycliffe, another spreader of heresy. He was teaching, as Wycliffe had, that truth can come to the Christian straight from the Bible without any popes or cardinals to tell him what he must believe. Some popes had been wicked, and any pope might be in error, Huss said. Whenever that was true, he declared, "I will not obey them even if you put before my eyes fire for the burning of my body."

Here—the authorities saw—was dangerous defiance. Huss was excommunicated. "We stand by you!" the people shouted. But some of the powerful men who at first had been on his side began to grow cool. And the king of Bohemia played him false. He let Huss be called before a great council of the Church in the city of Constance and did nothing to protect him. Huss was accused of heresy. Let him take back everything he had taught or face the awful death that would await a heretic. But Huss could not be moved. "It is better to die well than to live ill," he wrote from a prison cell to one of his friends. "One should not flinch."

And he did not flinch. "I write this," he said in another letter to his friends in Prague, "in prison and in chains, expecting to-morrow to receive sentence of death, full of hope in God that I shall not swerve from the truth." And when he was condemned and led to the place of execution, and the faggots were piled about the stake and the fire lighted, he said, "In the truth of that gospel which hitherto I have written, taught, and preached, I now joyfully die." And through the flames and smoke his voice was heard again in prayer.

The same council that condemned John Huss ordered also that the body of Wycliffe, buried in England, should be dug up, burned, and his ashes thrown into the river. They meant this as a disgraceful sign that all that Wycliffe had taught was done with now. But many Christian men began to think that as Wycliffe's ashes were carried from the Avon River to the Severn and by that to the sea,

> So Wyclif's words shall spread abroad
> Wide as the waters be.

And the fire that was lighted for the burning of John Huss's body did not die out with John Huss's death. It started a new fire of courage and devotion to truth which should flame up again in Bohemia and spread to other lands.

CHAPTER 22

TIMES OF CHANGE

T WAS in the year 1415 that John Huss was put to death. The period that had already begun by that time and that continued for the next hundred years and more is called in history the Renaissance, or the New Birth. For a new kind of life was being born in Europe. It was a life that seemed magnificent on the outside. But dangerous corruption was within it, and the very people who were building the new world they lived in were often the most abominable in their behavior.

The crusades had failed to win the Holy Land for a Christian kingdom, but they had had another and different result. Lands of the East which had been only far-off names before had grown familiar. Thousands of men from Europe had learned the ways by land and sea that led there. So the roads of the crusaders became trade routes. Italian cities, such as Venice at the head of the Asiatic Sea, grew rich and splendid from the commerce carried in their ships. They brought back from the East and sold in Europe the linens and silks, the rugs and tapestries, the dates and figs and spices, which men of the West had not known before. Not only in Italy but all over Europe, and especially in Germany and in the Low Countries on the North Sea, market towns and great commercial cities were growing up. Rich merchants became bankers also. Barons and bishops and popes borrowed money from them for the new buildings and the new luxuries that were now the fashion.

And it was not only the growth in wealth that made the times exciting. There was a thrilling recovery of knowledge that had been lost and almost forgotten, and that now broke upon the western world like sunrise after a long darkness. Scholars had begun to discover again records of the great thinkers and the great artists of ancient Greece. In 1453 the Turks captured

119

Constantinople, and men who had fled from the city before it fell brought with them precious manuscripts and works of art. Like the builders of the Tower of Babel, proud lords and prelates in the West began to think that there was nothing too magnificent for them to manage.

What was happening in other places was happening most of all in Rome. The popes had gradually brought it about that all disputes, lawsuits, and settlements in the Church anywhere had to be brought to Rome for final judgment, and there were endless fees and costs collected in the papal courts. Meanwhile the popes were compelling the first year's revenues of every newly appointed bishop to be sent to the pope, and heavy payments from rich monasteries and from churches and from ordinary people besides.

When Constantinople fell, the pope was Nicholas V. He was full of enthusiasm for the new learning, and he brought to Rome all the scholars, architects, and artists that he could get to come there. Popes who followed him for the next fifty years and more had this same enthusiasm, but the trouble with some of them was that this was all they had. Greed and self-indulgence corrupted them. Instead of being chief bishops of the Church, they were men of the world and indecent ones at that. Great buildings were going up in Rome, and artists like Michelangelo and Raphael were filling them with beauty. But the immoral lives of popes and scandals of the papal court were making men everywhere lose respect for the Church, which the popes had been supposed to represent. Early in the fourteenth century the great Italian poet Dante had written his *Divine Comedy*. In that supreme poem he gave a picture of conditions and peoples of his own times. He described an imagined journey among the souls of those who had died and were being punished for their sins, and bishops and popes were among those he called by name as being in the torments of hell.

In the city of Florence near the end of the century a Dominican monk, Savonarola, began to preach against the wickedness that was spreading through all Italy. The greatest church in Florence was jammed with the awed crowds who listened to his blazing words. One of the worst of the popes, Alexander VI, who had been the Cardinal Rodrigo Borgia, was on the papal throne. So Savonarola dared to demand that he should be deposed. But the power of the pope and of others who were afraid of so dangerous a preacher was too great. Savonarola was excommunicated. Then he was imprisoned, tortured, condemned, and burned at the stake in the public square of Florence.

It was not only a passionate preacher here and there, such as Savonarola, who wanted something better than the corruption that was spreading in the Church. The most famous scholar of the time, Erasmus of Rotterdam, wrote his scorching descriptions of what the popes were allowing to go on, though he was cautious enough to attack the papal court rather than the popes themselves as Savonarola had been bold to do. He said:

Those supreme Pontiffs who stand in the place of Christ, if they should try to imitate His life, that is, His poverty, His toil, His teaching, His cross, and His scorn of this world . . . what could be more dreadful! We ought not to forget that such a mass of scribes, copyists, notaries, advocates, secretaries, mule-drivers, grooms, money-changers, procurers, and gayer persons yet I might mention—that this whole swarm which now burdens (I beg your pardon, honors) the Roman See, would be driven to distraction.

And as for the monks:

The greater part of them have such faith in their ceremonies and human traditions, that they think one heaven is not reward enough for such great doings. . . . One will show his belly stuffed with every kind of fish; another will count up myriads of fasts, and make up for them all again by almost bursting himself at a single dinner. Another will bring forward such a heap of ceremonies that seven ships would hardly hold them. But Christ will interrupt their endless bragging.

Yet the common people of Europe had been accustomed, since before anyone could remember, to listen to what the Church taught and to do it. How they got their living day by day might depend upon themselves, but what would happen to their souls hereafter would depend entirely on the Church. The Church could open the way to heaven, or it could declare that one would go to hell. Also the Church taught that when a man died, he might not be ready yet to be either rewarded with heaven or condemned to hell. He would go instead to a middle place called purgatory, where he would be punished in torments for his sins; and the Church could determine how long he would stay there. So the people went to church, and they paid the priests for baptisms and for burials in holy ground. They went on pilgrimages to shrines that were supposed to be holy, especially if they had relics in them: the body of some saint who was buried there, or a piece of wood that was said to have come from the cross, or a piece of cloth that was advertised as having come from a robe of the Virgin Mary, or a bone of one of the Wise Men who had brought their gifts to Bethlehem. Say prayers in the right places, kiss the relics or the case that held them, give money to the Church for masses, and a man could get himself or somebody he loved out of purgatory sooner. That was what multitudes believed. But now even those who were simple folk and had no schooling were beginning to be restless and to ask questions.

Also for a long time there had been little companies of Christians in Germany and in the Low Countries who called themselves the Friends of God and Brethren of the Common Life. They were not separated from the Church, but they had quiet meetings of their own, to pray and to try to understand the gospel. Out of one of these groups came a book that numberless people were to read and treasure. It was *The Imitation of Christ,* and its message was what those who truly wanted to be Christians were hungry to receive, as they read in it words like these:

"Come unto Me, all ye that labour and are heavy laden, and I will refresh you," saith the Lord. . . . These are Thy words, O Christ the eternal Truth. . . . Because, therefore they are Thine and true, they are all thankfully and faithfully to be received by me. . . . I cheerfully receive them from Thy mouth, that they may be the more deeply implanted in my heart.

Thus the time had come when someone in Europe might speak the word that would shake the Church of Rome from top to bottom. The man who was to speak it did appear, but he did not come from some great place as might have been expected. He came from among the peasants, a miner's son. And in his early manhood he was only a monk who seemed at first too obscure for anyone to notice.

CHAPTER 23

A NEW DISCOVERER OF THE GOSPEL

T WAS on the tenth of November, 1483, that a son was born to Hans and Margaretta Luther in the little German town of Eisleben. In the village church he was christened Martin.

Like most of the German peasantry Hans Luther and his wife were simple folk who took their religion in the way the Church had taught them. The boy Martin learned the creed and the Ten Commandments. But what if he broke some of the commandments or sinned in some other way? In the church in a nearby town where he went to school he used to look at a stained-glass window that showed Christ, stern-faced and terrible, sitting on a rainbow with a sword in his hand coming to judge sinners in the last day. Over the altar was the carving of a ship that represented the Church carrying souls to heaven. Where would he be? the boy wondered. Standing before the sword of the Judge? Or somehow in the ship with the saved souls?

By nature Martin Luther was full of life and spirit. He did well enough in school. He liked people, and they liked him. He played the lute and loved to sing. Meanwhile his father had prospered, and Martin could enter the University of Erfurt, the most famous then in Germany. He was getting ready to be a lawyer.

But all the while something deep down was troubling him. Like all other people of the time he believed in devils—devils that were as real as they looked in the stained-glass windows that showed them dragging off the wicked at the judgment day to the flames of hell. What if the devils were reaching out for his soul?

From what the Church taught, it seemed to him that the surest hope of heaven must be in the monasteries, where men gave their whole lives to prayer and to hearing Mass. Then one day

124

to the amazement of his companions in the university he decided. Some say that he had been terrified by a bolt of lightning in a thunderstorm and had cried out to God and to the saints, "Save me, and I will become a monk!" However it was that he made the vow, he carried it out.

His father was shocked and angry. He had been ambitious for this son of his to practice law and prosper. But Martin Luther could not be persuaded now to what his father hoped for. He knocked for admission at the gates of one of the strictest of the monastic orders, the Augustinians. From then on he would be bound by the vow of poverty. He would wear rough garments, eat sparse food, spend his days in labor or in the round of prayers that went on also into the night, and live his life behind the cloister walls.

Martin Luther thought that now he could be at peace with God. If to be a monk was to win salvation, he would go the whole way of faithfulness. He prayed and fasted beyond what any rule required. He wore a hair shirt next to his flesh. In his cell he scourged himself as penance for what he thought to be his sins. He went to his father-confessor so often for confession that the priest lost patience and told him to stop coming until he had something serious to confess. But still Luther's soul was tormented by the fear that he was a sinner condemned by God.

Then one day a new light broke upon him, which in its results was like a miracle. He was reading the words of the apostle Paul, "The just shall live by faith." So that was the real meaning of the gospel! Life would come not by works but by faith. Not by what a man had to try to do but by what the love of God had done already. Not by fastings and scourgings and by all sorts of desperate efforts supposed to win God's mercy, but by the mercy that was declared in Christ. Jesus was not most of all the Judge; he was the Savior. He, Martin Luther, poor sinner though he might be, through the love of Jesus crucified was already saved!

Now a new chapter of life began for Luther. The head of the monastery sent him to be a lecturer and preacher in the recently founded university at Wittenberg. Students crowded to listen to him. Here was a man who had something to say that was full of hope and power.

All this while Luther was a dutiful son of the Church. It did not occur to him that he could come into collision with popes or bishops or anyone else who was supposed to be serving God.

Always, though, Luther was a man of strong feelings. His anger could blaze up against anything that seemed to him false and wrong. Now something happened that did make his anger blaze and light such a fire as he had never dreamed of.

There had grown up in the Church what was called the doctrine of indulgences. It was said that the saints and holy men had been so good—beyond what God required of ordinary people— that they had laid up a credit account in heaven. The pope could draw on that credit account for the benefit of sinners. If they did all that the priests told them to do, and gave money to the Church, the pope could declare that God would give them some of the extra forgiveness that the saints had won. Then they could be promised that they would not have to spend so many years in purgatory. That was the meaning of the indulgence.

The pope was Leo X. His family had got him made a cardinal when he was only thirteen, and being pope meant to him a chance to live in luxury and to enjoy the excitements of the Renaissance. The one thing about the Church that interested him most was building the immense St. Peter's Cathedral in Rome. But for that he needed money, and he looked around for ways to get it.

In Germany, Albert of Brandenburg was already bishop of two places. He wanted also to be archbishop of Mainz. The pope said he would make him an archbishop if Albert would send twelve thousand ducats to Rome. That was a huge sum, and Albert said it was too much. He might raise seven thousand ducats. Not enough, the pope said. Finally they agreed on ten thousand. But how would Albert get together as much as that or pay back the bankers if he borrowed it? The answer hit upon was indulgences. The pope would send a preacher into Germany to stir the people up about what the indulgences would do. The money the people would bring to pay for them should come part to the pope and part to Albert.

The man whom the pope sent was a Dominican monk named John Tetzel. His one idea about selling the indulgences was to use ways that he had already found out would work. He would come to a town, set up a stand in the public square with the sign of the pope above it, and begin a thundering sermon to the people who crowded around to listen. Here *they* were, he said, and down in purgatory were their fathers and mothers or somebody else in their families who had died. What would they do? Do nothing? Leave those they ought to love and pity in fire and torment? Or set them free through the pope's indulgence? Step up, then, and bring their contributions. "When the money clinks in the box," said Tetzel, "a soul flies out of purgatory!"

Tetzel came to a town close to Wittenberg. Many of the Wittenberg people went to hear him and bought their indulgences. Luther was indignant. Tetzel and his preaching looked to him like a coarse fraud. No true gospel was in it. Nothing but a trading on people's ignorance and fears.

What could he do? Well, he could bring the whole matter to everybody's notice, so that people could stop and think and make up their minds. He wrote down his own opinions, which he would be ready to defend in a debate. There was a long list of them, ninety-five in all. These ninety-five theses, as they were called, Luther nailed on the door of the castle church of Wittenberg, which was a sort of bulletin board that was read by the teachers and students of the university and the people of the town.

In his theses Luther said that although the pope had authority over the Church on earth, he had no authority over purgatory. He said that if any man was truly sorry for his sins and trusted in God's mercy through Christ, he would be forgiven, so there was no need of any indulgence from the pope. But if the pope thought he did have power to grant indulgences, why didn't he *give* them instead of having Tetzel get money out of the poor German people?

It was on the eve of All Saints' Day, October 31, 1517, that

Luther nailed his theses on the door of the church in Wittenberg. He did not know it then, but by that act he had begun a new chapter in history that would be called the Reformation.

Before this time the printing press had been invented, and therefore ideas could be circulated in a way that had never been possible in earlier centuries. Luther's theses were printed and spread all over Germany. Luther himself was astonished at the stir they made. But what he had said was exactly what thousands in Germany, among both the princes and the common people, had been waiting for someone to say in words that everybody could understand. They were beginning to have their doubts about this business of indulgences. What they had *no* doubt about was that they were tired of having money for indulgences go out of Germany to pay for the popes' buildings in Rome.

Luther did not suppose at first that he had done anything dangerous. He had meant to attack Tetzel, not to attack the Church. Pope Leo, when he was told of what had happened, waved it off as something not worth bothering about. "Some drunken monk," he said. "When he is sober, he will talk differently."

But Luther's words were having results. People stopped buying the indulgences. Money was not coming in. Albert of Brandenburg was annoyed. He wrote to the pope about it. Now the pope was annoyed too. Something had to be done.

The pope ordered the head of the Augustinian Order to make Luther stop talking. He also sent representatives up into Germany to set things straight. But they came back with disturbing news. They said that all over Germany people were saying that Luther was right and that they stood back of him.

Still Luther did not want to think of himself as anything but an obedient son of the Church. He thought that the pope, when he understood that there had been abuses, such as Tetzel's preaching, would want to correct them.

But then Luther was challenged to a debate by the learned scholar Dr. John Eck. In that debate Eck set out to show that it was not just Tetzel whom Luther was attacking. It was not Tetzel but the pope who had proclaimed the indulgence. It was the pope who claimed power from God to set souls free from purgatory. Luther was preaching notions that he claimed to have found for himself from reading the Gospels. But it was the Church, and the pope as the head of it, that had the only authority to say what the truth was. If Luther denied that, he was making the same denial that had caused the Church to burn John Huss at the stake. He was like John Huss. He was a heretic.

"God forbid!" was Luther's answer. He had never imagined that his thought was moving in the way of Huss. Heretic was an ugly word. How could he be like Huss?

But as the debate went on, Luther saw that he had to go further than he had thought at first. He was appealing to the Bible over the heads of popes and councils. He was saying that forgiveness came through what Christ had suffered once for all on the cross and not through any new miracle in the Mass. He dared even to say that popes had been in error and could be in error again. Then it was the duty of a Christian to follow his conscience no matter what popes and priests might say. A man could be saved by Christ alone without any machinery of the Church.

There was no doubt as to what had happened now. Luther was in defiance of the pope. Henceforth there would not be just debates. Rome would let loose its punishments.

The pope put Luther under the ban. This meant that he was forbidden to preach and teach. If he disobeyed, he would be excommunicated. Luther was ready with his answer. He put up a public notice inviting all in Wittenberg who held to the truth of the gospel to assemble by the Chapel of the Holy Cross outside the city gates. Before the excited crowd that gathered there Luther appeared. In his hand was a copy of the pope's ban. A fire was lighted, and Luther threw the pope's ban into it. Popes had burned heretics. Now Luther burned this paper and what he dared call its false claim of the authority of the pope.

CHAPTER 24

ONE LONELY MONK AMONG THE MIGHTY

LL GERMANY watched to see what would come next. Certainly this one monk was in deadly peril. His own prince, Duke Frederick of Saxony, liked him for his honesty and courage, and would protect him as far as he could. But the forces against him might be too great.

The newly elected head of the Holy Roman Empire, the Emperor Charles V, part German but part Spaniard, was presiding over his first diet—an assembly of all the princes and other rulers of the states making up the empire. The session was being held in the city of Worms. The young emperor had heard with anger of the upstart monk who was setting himself up against authority. When Luther's case was brought up, he wanted to condemn him at once and get rid of him. "The emperors before me were true sons of the Catholic Church," he said, "and I would rather lose all my lands and even my life than go against the Christian faith." But Duke Frederick and a few others insisted that Luther be allowed to appear and plead his cause.

From Wittenberg therefore Luther set out on a journey from which he knew that he might never come back. He had written to Duke Frederick:

You ask me what I shall do if I am called by the emperor. I will go even if I am too sick to stand on my feet. . . . If violence is used, as well it may be, I commend my cause to God. . . . This is no time to think of safety. I must take care that the gospel is not brought into contempt by our fear to confess and seal our teaching with our blood.

On the morning of April 16, 1521, a watchman on the city wall of Worms blew his horn to announce that Luther was approaching. With three companions he rode in a cart that the town of Wittenberg had provided for him. When it rolled into the

130

streets of Worms, great crowds of people poured out of their houses to surround Luther and to escort him to his lodging.

The next day the herald of the emperor came to inform Luther that he was to appear that afternoon in the great audience room of the bishop's palace, where the emperor was staying. At the appointed time Luther set out for the palace, through streets so packed with people that he had difficulty getting through. As he went along, the old warrior Frundsberg, the most famous soldier in Germany, clapped him on the shoulder and said: "My poor monk! my little monk! Thou art on thy way to make a stand as I and many of my knights have never done in our toughest battles. If thou art sure of the justice of thy cause, then forward in the name of God, and be of good courage: God will not forsake thee."

Luther had need of courage. When he entered the great hall of the palace, lighted with torches, he found it jammed so that there was no more standing room. On his throne sat Charles V. Around him in the diet were the powerful lords of the empire, most of whom looked at him with hard and hostile faces. A solitary figure in his drab monk's robe, he stood against a background of velvet and ermine, silken banners and glittering arms.

As he came through the door, Luther saw an old friend and spoke to him. Then he paused. The special representative of the pope, Aleander, wrote afterward: "The fool entered smiling; he looked slowly round and his face sobered."

The charge against him was read. On a table were copies of his book. Had he written those?

Yes, he had.

Would he now confess that they were full of heresy and falsehood? Let him answer yes or no.

Luther asked to be allowed overnight to make up his mind. The next day he stood again in the center of the great hall, facing Charles V and the members of the diet.

"Most serene Lord Emperor, most illustrious princes, most clement lords," he began, "I now present myself obediently at the time set yesterday evening for my appearance." He asked

their patience if he should use any wrong titles in speaking to them, for he said he had not been brought up in palaces.

"As for myself," he went on, "I can bear witness to this point only—that hitherto I have taught and written in simplicity of mind, having in view only the glory of God and the sincere instruction of Christian believers."

As to his books he pointed out that there were many of them and that even his enemies admitted that some things in them were true. How, then, could he take them all back?

The examiner was impatient. Let him give a straight answer. Let him say whether he was setting himself up against the Church's teaching or whether he was not.

Very well, said Luther, he would answer simply. "I believe in neither popes nor councils alone; for it is perfectly well established that they have frequently erred, as well as contradicted themselves. Unless then I shall be convinced by the testimony of scriptures or by clear reason, I must be bound by those scriptures which have been brought forward by me; yes, my conscience has been taken captive by these words of God. I cannot revoke anything, nor do I wish to; since to go against one's conscience is neither safe nor right. Here I stand. I cannot do otherwise! God help me. Amen."

Here was plain defiance! The diet was in tumult. Some of the Spaniards moved toward Luther with furious threats. But German knights ringed him round and escorted him out of the diet.

Luther was ordered to leave Worms and go back to Wittenberg. He was promised safety only until the diet gave its judgment.

Then suddenly the angry report spread in the streets of Wittenberg that Luther had been kidnaped. Armed men had seized him on the road. He had disappeared, no one knew where. He might be in prison. He might be already dead.

But actually it was his friends who had him. The wise old Duke Frederick had ordered some of his knights to lie in wait on Luther's road to take him and carry him off. They were to hide him somewhere without letting even the duke himself know where he was, so that he could not answer questions. And there was mortal need to hide him. For now the emperor had issued a condemnation of Luther and of any who might be his followers. If he was found, he could expect the same fate that had come to Huss.

For a year Luther was within the fortified walls of the castle of the Wartburg. While he was there, he translated the New Testament into German. Perhaps it was then also that he wrote what became the battle hymn of the Reformation, the great hymn that begins:

> A mighty fortress is our God,
> A bulwark never failing.

But meanwhile things were not going well at Wittenberg. Melanchthon, the brilliant young professor at the university and Luther's beloved friend, managed to get a message to him. The movement against old abuses in the Church was out of control. Rioting had broken out. Statues of the Virgin and saints were being smashed in the churches and priests and monks assaulted in the streets.

Luther left the castle and went back to Wittenberg. He knew that he did it at peril of his life. But his preaching and his presence among the people restored order in the town. And no actual move was made to arrest him. The pope could excommunicate—and he had excommunicated Luther—but only what was called the "secular arm" could punish. The pope would have to get the emperor or one of the princes in Germany to act. But Charles V had trouble in other quarters. Also there were other princes in Germany besides the old Duke Frederick who would stand by Luther. There could be danger to the empire in provoking them too far.

In the years following, Germany was continually on the edge of division and religious war. A diet which met at Speyer in 1526 allowed the preaching of the Reformation in the territories of those princes who favored it. But three years later the emperor had this forbidden. Then the members of the diet who were on Luther's side drew up a proclamation of their faith and a ringing protest against the effort of Charles V to overrule their freedom of belief. So the word "Protestant" arose. The Protestant princes formed a league, which the emperor did not quite dare to challenge.

Meanwhile Luther was arranging the life and worship of the churches that looked to him for leadership. He had never meant at first to form a new church, but to get rid of abuses in the one Church into which he and all other Christians had been born. But now the break had come. He would have no more to do with the popes in Rome. He would change the practices—such as the sale of indulgences, the worship of relics, the use of the Mass as if it were a kind of saving magic—that he held to be corruptions of the gospel. The Bible should be preached, the services should be in the people's own German tongue instead of in Latin, and in the Mass the people should be given not only the bread but also the wine that the Church of Rome had let nobody but the priests receive. But except where there was reason to change, he kept what was familiar and accustomed: ordination of men as ministers and bishops, the ancient books of prayer, clergy vestments, altar lights.

In the early centuries, when the Roman world was breaking up, there was reason for monasteries. Now Luther said that it was wrong for so many of the best people to be taken out of regular life. Moreover, he would put an end to the rule that Rome had set up that the clergy should not marry. He himself was no longer a monk, and he married Katherine von Bora, who with some other nuns had left her convent when the Reformation began. They had three sons and two daughters; and it was for his own children first that Luther wrote the lovely songs that numberless children have sung, such as the Christmas carol which contains the stanza:

> Ah, dearest Jesus, Holy Child,
> Make thee a bed, soft, undefiled,
> Within my heart, that it may be
> A quiet chamber kept for Thee.

For twenty-five years after the diet of Worms, Luther lived and worked. Always he was in danger; and if the pope could have had his way, Luther would have been burned as a heretic, as John Huss was. But so many of the princes of Germany had rallied to his side that neither the pope nor the emperor could arrest him.

A man of a great, warm heart, Luther had also a passionate temper. He could make grievous mistakes, the worst of which was when he urged the German princes to put down without mercy the outbreaks of violence of poor people who started the Peasants' Revolt. But he had tried all his life to be a servant of God. When he fell sick in what was to be his final illness, it was when he had gone in bitter winter weather to preach in the little town where he was born. He stopped his sermon suddenly and said, "This and much more is to be said about the gospel; but I am too weak, and we will close here."

CHAPTER 25

OTHER CHAMPIONS OF THE NEW FAITH

HIS AND much more is to be said about the gospel" were the last words of Luther in the pulpit. More *was* being said by others who carried on the message of the Reformation.

A few months after Luther was born in Germany, Ulrich Zwingli was born in Switzerland. He went to the universities of Vienna and of Basle, and he belonged to those who were called the Humanists. These were the men, like the great scholar Erasmus of Rotterdam, who were keen to discuss all the questions that had been raised by the new learning. Zwingli was never a monk, as Luther was; but he became a parish priest and went about his ordinary duties among the people. What interested him most was studying. He learned Greek and Hebrew, so that he might read the Old Testament and the New Testament in the languages in which they were written.

But like other humanists he recognized superstitions that had grown up in the Church and was out of patience with them. The town in which he was priest had a shrine to which many people came on pilgrimage. Zwingli grew disgusted with the superstitious belief in the power of relics and with the whole idea that people gained virtue by saying their prayers at particular shrines. And what roused him most was when a seller of indulgences came from the pope to Switzerland, not long after Tetzel had gone to Martin Luther's Germany.

When he was still a young man, Zwingli became the preacher at the great Minster Church in the city of Zurich. Now he began to instruct the people out of the Bible. Crowds flocked to hear him, because he was giving them knowledge they had never heard of. He was preaching also what Luther had dared to preach in Germany—that it is the Bible, and not popes or councils, that is the first and last word of truth for Christians. The

137

Bible alone, he said, "contains perfectly all piety and the whole rule of life."

An attack of the plague swept over Switzerland. Zwingli fell ill of it and nearly died. When he recovered, his preaching became the more urgent. The rule that all priests should be unmarried had no basis in the Bible, he declared. All that it did was to lead to immorality. He preached against prayers to the saints. He went further than Luther in sweeping out of the churches things he said ought not to be there, because there was no word about them in the Bible. There must be no more images of Christ or the Virgin or the saints, no more crosses, no more organs. He attacked the Romish doctrine that in the Mass the bread and wine were turned into the body and blood of Christ. He and Luther agreed in that. But when the two great reformers finally met each other in the city of Marburg, they could not agree as to what *did* happen in the Holy Communion. Luther insisted that Christ's presence was there in some special way in the bread and wine. Zwingli said the service was a service of remembrance. So the Lutheran Church in Germany and the Reformed Church in Switzerland went their separate ways.

Zwingli believed more than Luther did in the rule of the people. Luther was willing to have a country under the rule of its prince. Zwingli wanted the state, and also the Church, to be regulated by representatives elected by the people. The authorities of the part of Switzerland of which Zurich was the center stood by Zwingli, and the changes he wanted were carried out in the churches. War broke out with other parts of Switzerland that held to the Church of Rome. Zwingli went as a chaplain with the Reformation army into battle. He was struck down, killed, and his body afterward cut to pieces by the hangman. But beside the road where he fell is a monument to Zwingli which bears these words: "They may kill the body, but not the soul."

In Zurich there were others who broke away from the Church of Rome. They felt that Luther and Zwingli had gone only halfway toward having a Church that would be according to the gospel. The Church, they said, ought to be made up only of true believers. The state authorities should have no control over it, and members of the Church should have no part in state affairs. They should not hold office, nor take any oaths, nor bear arms. And in order to be in this Church that people would belong to only because they chose to and not just because they were born in a particular family or a particular country, everybody who had received what had been called baptism as a baby must be truly baptized now that he was old enough to understand. Baptism of children, they said, was nothing but a false invention. The one real baptism in the sight of God was when a grown person stood up and declared his faith. So some of them baptized one another. Therefore they were called Anabaptists, which meant the "baptized again."

Not only the Catholics but the followers of Luther and Zwingli looked upon the Anabaptists with horror. It seemed to them that here were men who were breaking loose with wild ideas that would destroy all law and order. And some of the Anabaptists did stir ignorant people up to dangerous excitement, so that anybody who was called an Anabaptist was liable to ferocious persecution. But many of them were people of pure devotion and of great heroism.

Among them was a converted priest named Menno Simons. His followers in Holland were known as the Mennonites. They practiced among themselves a love and charity like that of Christians in the New Testament times. When they were persecuted, they endured it without asking that any earthly power should protect them. "Soon shall come the day of our refreshing, and all the tears shall be wiped from our eyes," said Menno Simons. "Praise God and lift up your heads, ye who suffer for Jesus' sake."

The message of the Reformation came into France also. But the followers of the pope, who now were called the Catholics, hunted down the Protestants wherever they were found.

From a Catholic family of France came a man who was to

rank with Luther and Zwingli as one of the great reformers—though most of his life, and his death, would be outside his own country. His name was John Calvin.

In his youth Calvin was on the way to becoming a priest. Then he began instead to study law. At the universities of Paris and Orléans he was such a brilliant scholar that he was called on to lecture if the regular professors were away. Meanwhile he was learning Greek and reading the New Testament. Also he was beginning to read the writings of Luther that had been brought, at the risk of those who dared to have them, into France.

Like the humanists and other men who were not afraid to think, Calvin already saw that there were many abuses that needed to be corrected in the Church. But now he became convinced of more than that. Luther was right. There had to be a whole new understanding of the gospel, based directly on the New Testament and not on the partly corrupted practices of the Church of Rome.

Soon therefore Calvin joined one of the little groups of Protestants that were secretly growing up in France. Twice he was arrested and briefly imprisoned. Switzerland was being torn by religious war, but some parts of it at least seemed safer than France. Calvin made his way to the city of Basle. What he wanted to do was to settle down in quiet to study and to write. And he did write. When he was only twenty-six years old, he published the book that has put its mark on Protestant thought more than almost any other book ever written, his *Institutes of the Christian Religion.*

On a journey Calvin had to stop in Geneva. There to his inn came an overpowering visitor. This was William Farel, who was already preaching the reformed gospel in the city. Farel was a man of burning conviction, with a tremendous voice. Once when he was preaching in a church, Roman Catholic opponents set all the tower bells ringing; but Farel made a great crowd hear him through all the din of the bells. Now he besieged Calvin with passionate argument. Calvin's duty, Farel said, was to leave Basle and come to work in Geneva. Farel made Calvin feel that not to listen might be a dreadful sin of disobedience. Calvin said afterward that it was "as if God had stretched forth his hand upon me from on high to arrest me."

So Calvin did come to Geneva, and he and Farel worked together. Now there was to be an end to the quiet that Calvin had longed for. The city council that governed Geneva had voted to allow no more authority of Rome. The Reformation gospel could be preached in the churches. But that did not mean that all the people were ready yet for a new kind of Christian life. They were ready to get rid of sellers of indulgences and and of having money go out of Switzerland to Rome. But this did not make them welcome preachers who wanted to reform their morals. Geneva was a turbulent city with plenty of drunkenness, gambling, and loose living generally.

It was not long before rioting broke out against Farel and Calvin. They were preaching in plain words about the sins that people had to stop committing if they were to come to church. There was one man whose evil living was so notorious that Farel and Calvin gave notice that they would forbid his coming to Communion. On an Easter Sunday he was there. An angry, crowded congregation watched to see what would happen. Calvin stood up and announced that if any unworthy person dared to try to come to the Communion, there would be no Communion for anyone. And there was none. He closed the service.

Calvin and Farel were followed through the streets with threats and curses. The city council met and banished them from Geneva.

But conditions in Geneva went from bad to worse, and people began to change their minds. After three years they appealed to Calvin to come back. So he returned, though Farel, who was working in another city, would not be with him again.

For the rest of his life, until he died worn out by labors in which he never spared himself, Calvin made Geneva a Reformation stronghold. Protestants persecuted in other lands fled there for refuge, and preachers went out from it to carry the beliefs they had heard preached and seen practiced in Geneva.

Religion was no empty form or easy word for Calvin. He wanted all Geneva to live seven days a week according to what he believed to be God's commandments. He started schools where children would be taught the catechism which he wrote for them. He wanted the laws of the Church to determine the laws of the city. Every congregation was governed by its elected elders; and the elders met together in an assembly called the presbytery, which made the rules for the whole Church. Thus arose the name Presbyterian for those Christian churches in many countries that trace their history back to Geneva and to Calvin.

Geneva was on the border of France, and France was still fiercely Roman Catholic. So were parts of Switzerland. Calvin believed that if the Church in Geneva was to live, it had to be disciplined like an army of the Lord. Its people must be like the Israelites in Old Testament times when they were on guard against the Canaanites and the Midianites and other enemies round about. The people of the Reformation were the new chosen people, inheritors of the promise God had made to Abraham. And if they were to deserve his promise, they must completely obey his law.

Therefore Calvin tried to order life in Geneva according to what he thought was the pattern of holiness. There were stern punishments not only for the wicked but also for the careless and the easygoing. A man could be fined or imprisoned for playing dice for a bottle of wine or for laughing in church or going to sleep during a sermon, for doing anything he was not supposed to do on the Sabbath or for wearing more showy clothes than were allowed.

It was a grim and stern kind of obedience that Calvin required. It could not be kept up for long. But in a time of danger it created men who had convictions and a courage that nothing could shake. From Calvin's teaching they believed in a God whose will is sovereign and whose purpose nothing can resist. They had no fear except the fear of being disobedient. And when they had set themselves to be faithful to what they thought was the will of God, they were not afraid of the face of any man.

CHAPTER 26

CONFLICTS IN ENGLAND AND IN SCOTLAND

HE REFORMATION came to England soon after it had begun in Germany and in Switzerland, but with a difference. It was not so violent. And in the end more of the old ways and customs of the Church were left unchanged.

King Henry VIII of England was married to Catherine of Aragon, a princess from Spain. They had had six children, but all of them had died as babies except one daughter. Henry wanted a son who would succeed him on the throne. He thought he might have one if he could get rid of Catherine and marry another wife.

Henry tried to persuade the pope to agree that he might do this. His argument was that actually he ought not to have been married to Catherine in the first place. Catherine had been married to Arthur, Henry's oldest brother. Arthur had died, and she was married then to Henry. Henry claimed now that marriage to a brother's widow was against the law of the Church. The previous pope had given permission to set aside that law. But no pope could have had a right to do that, said Henry. His marriage to Catherine therefore was no real marriage, but only a living in sin. Consequently—he claimed—the present pope ought to declare that he was not married at all.

The matter was discussed in Rome. Popes had set aside marriages in similar cases before. It was possible that the pope who was then ruling, Clement VII, would do what Henry wanted. But he was caught between two dangers. On the one hand, he did not want to make an enemy of the king of England. But on the other hand, Catherine of Aragon, the queen whom Henry wanted to be rid of, was the aunt of Charles V, emperor of the Holy Roman Empire. Already Charles had had a dispute with the pope, and at that very moment Charles's army was at Rome.

The pope did not dare give him a new cause for anger. So after a long time of doing nothing either way, the pope finally issued a decree forbidding Henry to marry somebody else and declaring that he must treat Catherine as his rightful queen.

Henry was indignant. He would show the pope who was master. He put Catherine away and married the young Anne Boleyn, with whom he had fallen in love and who, if she were his queen, he hoped might bear him a son. The whole dispute had been no credit either to him or to the pope.

Now the question was what would happen to the Church in England.

If the bishops and clergy and the nobility and the people of England generally had stood with the pope, there might have been rebellion. But for a long time they had been growing restless. More than a hundred years earlier Geoffrey Chaucer in his *Canterbury Tales* had held up the lazy and dishonest friar and monk to ridicule. John Wycliffe had denounced corruption in the Church and had sent out his poor preachers to teach the people directly from the Bible. And many who thought Wycliffe was too dangerous, and meant to be nothing but good Catholics, were restless under the pope's claims of authority. They were Englishmen, and they did not like to have Italian popes demand that so many matters in England must be brought to Rome for judgment. So when Convocation met, which was the assembly of the bishops and clergy of England, it passed a resolution that the "bishop of Rome hath no more authority in this realm than any other foreign potentate." And Parliament passed an act that the king should be considered the "singular protector, the only and supreme lord, and as far as is permitted by the law of Christ, the supreme head of the Church."

At first there seemed little change in the Church that touched most people's belief and worship. Henry broke up the monasteries and seized their wealth. He hunted down anyone who defended the pope, including the brave Sir Thomas More, who was executed in the tower of London. But otherwise England could go on being Catholic. A few years earlier, when Martin Luther had been condemned by the diet at Worms, Henry had written an insulting pamphlet against him; and the grateful Pope Leo X had awarded Henry the title "Defender of the Faith." Henry saw no reason to think that refusing to obey Leo's successor should make him any more sympathetic to Luther or any less a "Defender of the Faith."

But once the tie with Rome was broken, the spirit of the Reformation began to spread in England. At the universities of Cambridge and Oxford, Luther's works were read and men said to one another, "Here is the real gospel." Some also went from England to Switzerland and came back with the teachings of Zwingli, and later those of Calvin. Most important of all, Englishmen began to study the scriptures in their own language.

The man above all others who made that possible was William Tyndale. Born about 1492, and educated at Oxford and at Cambridge, he had mastered both Hebrew and Greek. Thus he had the scholar's ability to translate the Old and New Testaments directly from the languages in which they were written, and he had also a concern for human souls that roused in him a passionate purpose to make the Word of God known to all the people. Risking—as he well knew—the hostility of those who were most powerful in church and state, he set to work on his translation. To a church leader who challenged him he wrote this reply: "If God spare my lyfe, ere many yeares I wyl cause a boye that dryveth the plough shall know more of the scripture than thou doest!"

But it became too dangerous in England for Tyndale to stay there. He went to Germany, and there he finished his English translation of the New Testament and at length was able to get it printed. Copies of it were smuggled into England and read with eager excitement by men who now for the first time in English history were looking at a part of the Bible printed in the language that they knew.

To the king and to the bishops of the church this circulation of the Bible was a defiance of authority. All the copies of Tyndale's Testament that could be discovered were seized and burned by order of the Bishop of London outside St. Paul's Cathedral. But the bishop did not know that the London merchant Augustine Packynton, through whom he got hold of most of the books he burned, and whom he paid handsomely for delivering them, was a friend of Tyndale's. So the more books the bishop burned, the more money went back to Tyndale to print more books.

But while thus his work succeeded, Tyndale himself was in mortal danger. Enemies pursued him in Germany and then in Belgium. Before he could finish the translation also of the Old Testament, he was arrested, imprisoned near Brussels, and in 1536 brutally strangled and his body burned.

But the bringing of the Bible to the English people, which Tyndale gave his life for, did not stop with his death. Even before this, Miles Coverdale and other men in England had begun to carry on his work. And they found a patron to help them. After Henry VIII had broken with the pope, Thomas Cranmer, who had been of most help to the king in divorcing Catherine of Aragon, became Archbishop of Canterbury and thus the highest figure in the English Church. Cranmer recognized the value of an English Bible for an English church and urged it on Henry and other political leaders. Only three years after Tyndale's death an order went out that every parish church must have a Bible in the native tongue.

Henry died in 1547 after a brutal reign in the course of which he had married six wives and had one son. This son, a frail boy of ten, succeeded him as Edward VI. The boy's guardians were entirely in favor of an English church, and during his reign something was accomplished almost as important as translating the Bible into words everyone could understand. Thomas Cranmer took the Latin service books that contained the Mass and other forms of worship, and he made these over into the English *Book of Common Prayer*. Not only were the services now in the language of the people. They were reformed and purified. Cranmer meant to keep all that he believed to be a true part of the Church's great inheritance: the creeds, baptism and the Lord's Supper, the three orders of the ministry—bishops, priests, and deacons. But he left out what he believed to be the superstitions that had crept into the Church: the worship of the Virgin and the saints, belief in purgatory and in indulgences, the saying of Masses as though they were a kind of magic. And the beauty of the language in which he composed the *Book of Common Prayer* has made it one of the world's great books of devotion from that time on.

But the reign of Edward VI lasted only six years. When he died, he was succeeded by Mary, the daughter of Henry VIII and Catherine of Aragon. She was a fanatical follower of the pope, and all Protestants in England were now in deadly peril. Bishops and clergy who would not swear allegiance again to Rome were put out of office and some of them condemned to death. Two of them, Hugh Latimer, who had been bishop of Worcester, and Nicholas Ridley, bishop of London, were brought in chains to the town of Oxford and sentenced to be executed by burning at the stake. On the day when they were led toward it, Latimer turned and said to his companion, "Be of good comfort, Master Ridley, and play the man. We shall this day light such a candle by God's grace in England as I trust shall never be put out." And it was said of him that when the fires were lighted, "he received the flame as though embracing it."

In the same jail in Oxford from which Latimer and Ridley had been taken out to execution, there was another prisoner. This was the archbishop Thomas Cranmer. He knew what had happened to Latimer and Ridley, and he shrank from the awful thought of a death like theirs. Perhaps, as one who knew him wrote, he was "too fearful about what might happen to him." It may be, too, that he was confused as to his duty to the Church of England now that the queen and the country seemed to be turning back to submission to the pope. Whatever it was that moved him, what he did was to declare that he had been wrong in all his championship of the Reformation.

Now the queen in her fierce devotion to the Church of Rome had her moment of triumphant satisfaction. This Thomas Cranmer had been one of those who had aided her father, Henry VIII, to put away her mother, Catherine of Aragon. This same archbishop Cranmer had been the leading figure in bringing the Reformation gospel into the Church of England. Now he was humbled. Now he had confessed that he was in error; so, she thought, all England would be Roman Catholic.

But the faith and courage of the archbishop, though they had wavered, were not lost. He was to show them again in an act as astonishing as it was resolute. He had been taken to St. Mary's Church in Oxford and bidden to read there to all the people the denial of Protestant faith that he had made when he was put on trial. Instead he recited what had happened to him, and then to the amazed anger of his enemies he ended thus:

"And now, I am come to the great thing that troubleth my conscience more than any other thing that I ever said or did in my life, and that is the setting abroad of writings contrary to the truth; which here now I renounce and refuse, as things written with my hand, contrary to the truth which I thought in my heart, and writ for fear of death and to save my life if might be; and that is all such papers as I have written or signed since my degradation, wherein I have written many things untrue; and forasmuch as my hand offended in writing contrary to my heart, my hand when I come to the fire shall first be burned. And as for the pope, I refuse him as Christ's enemy and Antichrist with all his false doctrine."

"Stop the heretic's mouth, and take him away!" one of his accusers cried.

Then he was hurried, like Latimer and Ridley, to the stake. When the fire was lighted, he did what he said he would do. He put his right hand, which had written the words he now repented of, out into the flames, so that it would be burned first.

Mary lived only five years. When her reign ended, the power of the pope over England came also to its end. Mary was succeeded by Elizabeth, the daughter of Henry VIII and Anne Boleyn. Whatever else she believed or did not believe, there was one thing about which Elizabeth was determined. No control from Rome should ever come back to England.

Elizabeth's reign was one of the great periods in English history. Shakespeare was writing his plays in London. Drake and other sea captains were sailing out to attack the Spanish galleons laden with treasure from the new world in the West. Philip II, the Catholic king of Spain, gathered his ships of war into the great fleet that was called the Spanish Armada and sent it out to invade and conquer England. The English navy, aided by a storm, destroyed the Armada.

But the attack by the Armada was a sign of the dangers from enemies outside the realm that England had to take account of. Therefore Elizabeth was all the more concerned that there should be peace within. In the Church she wanted things to settle down in quietness. Worship was to be conducted according to the *Book of Common Prayer*. Services went on in the same ancient parish churches and cathedrals that the people had always known. Bishops who had been appointed before the time of Mary were to consecrate their successors and thus to keep the line unbroken. The Church of England was to be both Catholic and Protestant.

By this was meant that the Church would hold to the faith and ways of worship that were believed to be the inheritance of all Christians, but also it would have the freedom of conscience and the new knowledge of the Bible and of the gospel in it which the Protestant reformers had preached. Such was the Church of England as Elizabeth wanted it to be. And when in 1953 Elizabeth the Second was crowned, nearly four hundred years after Elizabeth the First, it was again in Westminster Abbey by the Archbishop of Canterbury; and the oath that she took was this:

The Archbishop:

Will you to the utmost of your power maintain the laws of God and the true profession of the gospel? Will you to the utmost of your power maintain in the United Kingdom the Protestant Reformed Religion established by law? Will you maintain and preserve inviolably the settlement of the Church of England, and the doctrine, worship, discipline and government thereof, as by law established in England?

The Queen:

All this I promise to do.

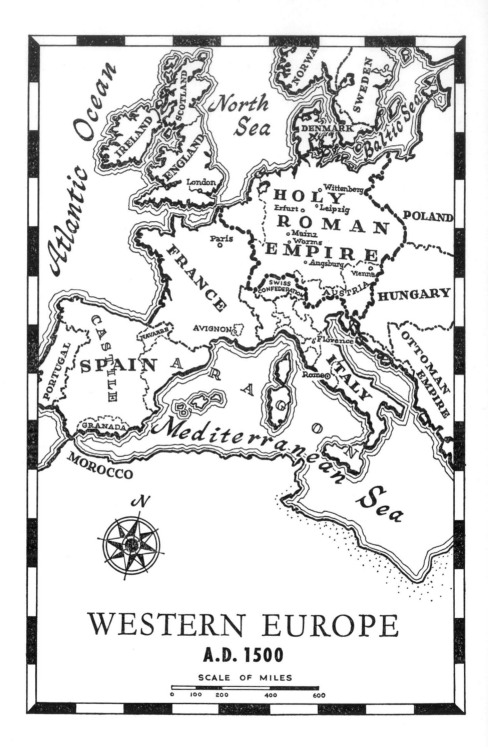

Atlantic Ocean

North Sea

IRELAND

SCOTLAND

ENGLAND

London

NORWAY

SWEDEN

DENMARK

Baltic Sea

HOLY ROMAN EMPIRE

Wittenberg

Erfurt   Leipzig

Mainz

Worms

Augsburg

Vienna

POLAND

Paris

FRANCE

SWISS CONFEDERATION

AUSTRIA

HUNGARY

PORTUGAL

CASTILE

SPAIN

NAVARRE

AVIGNON

ARAGON

Florence

ITALY

Rome

OTTOMAN EMPIRE

GRANADA

MOROCCO

Mediterranean Sea

N

WESTERN EUROPE
A.D. 1500

SCALE OF MILES

0   100   200   400   600

Meanwhile the Reformation had come in a more stormy way to Scotland in the north. Scotland was not joined to England then, but was a separate kingdom. Like England it had a ruling queen. She was a cousin of Elizabeth's. Her name was Mary; and in order not to confuse her with the other Mary, Elizabeth's sister, her name is written in history as Mary, Queen of Scots.

She had become queen when her father, James V of Scotland, died while she was a little child. She was sent to France, where later she was married to the young king Francis II. Scotland was governed by her mother, as regent in her name. Then when Mary was only sixteen, the king, her husband, suddenly died; and the next year she returned to Scotland.

Before Luther had begun to preach in Germany, Scotland had suffered from some of the same abuses from popes and bishops that were known in Europe. A few brave men began to preach the new faith which had come to them from Luther and Calvin. Resistance to them was savage. Two of the Reformation preachers, Patrick Hamilton and George Wishart, were burned at the stake. But others would defy the danger and bring the Reformation into Scotland.

Greatest among these was John Knox. He had graduated from one of the Scottish universities and become a priest. But George Wishart's preaching and his heroic death had made John Knox a defiant Protestant. He was arrested, taken to France, sentenced to nineteen months as a chained rower in a French galley. When he was released, he came to England while Edward VI was king. He fled when the Roman Catholic Mary succeeded to the English throne, and at length he got back to Scotland. Some of the nobility were swinging over to the Protestant side. The flaming preaching of John Knox persuaded more. In 1560 the Scottish Parliament adopted a Protestant confession of faith, denied the pope's authority, and forbade the saying of the Mass.

It was in the year after this that Mary of Scotland returned to be the reigning queen. She was young and beautiful and charming. She was a loyal Catholic, and she had her priest read Mass in the chapel of her palace.

"Shall that idol be suffered again to take place within this realm?" asked John Knox. "It shall not!" Others in Scotland were not so resolute. It looked as though the young queen might have her way. "I think," said Knox, "that there be some enchantment by which men are bewitched."

But the queen had no enchantment strong enough to change John Knox. Again and again he denounced to her face what he called the "vanity of the Papistical religion, and the deceit, pride and tyranny of that Roman Antichrist." When Mary found herself unable to match words and arguments with this terrible accuser, she burst into a storm of angry weeping. But Knox, with his grim conviction that he was the appointed spokesman of the truth of God, was too strong for her.

At length divisions in her kingdom forced the queen to seek refuge in England. Elizabeth had always distrusted her and been jealous of her beauty and her charm. Also Elizabeth had a secret fear that Mary might stir up treason in England and with the help of Roman Catholic France try to win Elizabeth's own throne. So she had Mary put under guard in a castle, then later tried, condemned, and executed.

Meanwhile John Knox had become more powerful in Scotland than most of its kings had been. He was like a voice of conscience that the whole country yielded to. He and his associates drew up a *Book of Discipline* to govern all who belonged to the Church, and a *Book of Common Order* to govern its life and worship after the pattern of Calvin in Geneva. From that time on most of the Scottish people would be rock-ribbed Presbyterians, and their kind of church would spread to the north of Ireland, into Wales, and to America beyond the sea.

CHAPTER 27

THE NEW ARMY OF THE POPES

HE LUTHERAN Church had been planted in parts of Germany and had spread into Sweden, Norway, and Denmark. The Reformed Church that had formed around Zwingli was in Zurich. Geneva was a stronghold of Calvinism. In France many had confessed the Reformation faith, though later a dreadful massacre in Paris on St. Bartholomew's Day killed most of their leaders, so that the Huguenots—as they were called—were almost destroyed. In England and in Scotland the authority of the pope was finished. But in the south of Europe most of the people still obeyed the Church of Rome.

And now the Catholics began to try to win back what they had lost. A council of the Church was called to meet in the city of Trent. Off and on the council held sessions for eighteen years. The better men there acknowledged among themselves that the lives of some of the popes had been scandalous and that reforms were needed in Rome. After that there would be no more immoral popes. But the council would not admit that Luther and the other reformers had been right in what they preached about the Christian faith. It declared that the traditions of the Church had as much authority as the Bible and that nobody had a right to pretend that he got out of the Bible anything different from what the Church had said was true. It said that those who die do go to purgatory and that indulgences can help them out of its punishments. And it declared that all Christians must obey the pope as the bishop of Rome, the "successor of St. Peter, Prince of the Apostles, and as the Vicar of Jesus Christ."

Once the Council of Trent had spoken and acted as it did, the division between the Church of Rome and the churches of the Reformation was complete.

And now the popes had new forces on their side. The greatest of these was the Society of Jesus, later to be called the Jesuits. Its founder was the Spaniard Ignatius Loyola. He was born in 1491, eight years after Luther was born in Germany and one year before Columbus sailed into the unknown western seas from Spain. And while Columbus was discovering a new world and Luther was creating a new church, Ignatius Loyola was to do more than any other man to defend the old religious world of Rome.

In his youth Ignatius was a soldier in a war between Spain and France. His leg was shattered by a cannon ball, and for a while it seemed that he would die. As he slowly recovered, there were long days when he could only lie and think. He began to meditate on the sins he had committed, on his soul, on what he ought to do. His chances of fighting in an army were finished. Well, could he be a soldier of Christ instead?

When he could travel, he made his way to the monastery of Montserrat, a famous place of pilgrimage. He put off the armor and laid down the weapons of a knight, put on sackcloth and made confession to a priest. Then he went away and found shelter in a monastery in another town. Doubts and struggles in his soul came to Ignatius Loyola as they had come to Martin Luther, but the answer that came to him was very different. He developed his *Spiritual Exercises,* which began with recollection of one's sins, went on to repentance and fasting and self-punishment, meditation on the sufferings of Christ, and then—above all—the giving of oneself in complete obedience to the service of the Church in submission to the pope.

All that Ignatius hoped and intended as to what he might do to strengthen the Church developed slowly. He went to Rome and made his way on pilgrimage to Palestine. He came back to Spain. Then for two years he studied at the University of Paris. There for the first time he drew a few other men about him; and they took the vows that monks took, of poverty, chastity, and obedience.

But none of the regular orders of monks seemed to Ignatius to be what was most needed. Those regular monks lived behind their monastery walls. For many periods each day they gathered in the choir to chant the psalms and say their prayers. Beautiful, Ignatius thought, for times of peace. But now, he thought, was a time of spiritual war. There needed to be servants of the Church who could go everywhere at any time. They could read their breviaries—the books of psalms and prayers—privately. They would not wear the dress of monks or live in monasteries. They would be missionaries to go wherever they were sent.

At length, when Ignatius was forty-nine years old, Pope Paul III gave to him and his few companions the pope's approval of their Society of Jesus. Ignatius himself had drawn up its constitution and its rules. It was to have in it the absolute discipline and obedience of an army. The Society should be everything, Ignatius said—the individual nothing. At its head should be a general, whose command was law. In the vow that each must take as he entered the Society, the new Jesuit must say: "I promise to Almighty God, before His Virgin Mother and the whole heavenly host, and to all standing by; and to thee, Reverend Father General of the Society of Jesus, holding the place of God, and to thy successors . . . , Perpetual Poverty, Chastity and Obedience." All this was to be under the supreme obedience rendered to the pope.

Once started, the Society of Jesus grew rapidly. It established schools and colleges, and developed great skill in teaching and preaching. Its members were the strongest influence in the Council of Trent. They fought against the new teachings of the Reformation. Ignatius Loyola said to his followers, "Let us all think the same way; let us all speak in the same manner if possible." That was what he wanted for the whole Church of Rome. And the Jesuits have stood for that same desire ever since.

With their fixed convictions and with their disciplined obedience the Jesuits were the shock troops of the popes against the Reformation. Protestant Churches had been planted in the north of Europe and in England and Scotland; but the Catholics held Italy and Spain and France and Austria, and they won back peoples in Poland, Bohemia, and Moravia, where at first the Reformation had been strong.

Nor was it only at home that the Jesuits labored. They were

heroic missionaries. Francis Xavier, one of Ignatius Loyola's earliest companions, went to India and to Japan and won many converts. He was trying to enter China when he died, and after his death other Jesuits did go in. And when the Spanish and French explorers and conquerors went to the new world, Jesuit missionaries went with them—into South America and Mexico, and among the Indians around the Great Lakes and in Canada.

So the Catholic Church was showing that there was much more in it than the luxury and corruption of Rome which had shocked the conscience and roused the wrath of Luther. It could produce men who were as devoted as the reformers were to what they believed was the truth of God and to what they held to be his purpose for the souls of men.

CHAPTER 28

PURITANS AND KINGS

N ENGLAND, after Elizabeth came to the throne, the Roman Catholics did not make much trouble. But those who were most opposed to them did.

Many Englishmen wanted the church in England to be more like Calvin's church in Geneva. They would rather have prayers that were not read out of a book. They wanted to get rid of vestments and the sign of the cross and other things that made the services look too much as they had looked before the Reformation. They would have liked to have each congregation free to follow its own ways. And they had no use for bishops.

When Elizabeth died, she was succeeded by the son of Mary, Queen of Scots. He had been James VI of Scotland. Now for the first time Scotland and England were under the same ruler, and his new title was James the First.

Because James had come from Scotland, and Scotland was Calvinist and Presbyterian, many of his new subjects expected that the king would be of that opinion. But actually James had a quite different idea. He liked authority for himself, and he thought that authority in the Church made authority in the state just that much more secure. "No bishop, no king," he said.

But great numbers of men and women in England did not like bishops. Also they wanted to get as far away as they could from anything that looked to them like Roman Catholicism. They wanted worship to be simple, and they believed in the kind of strictness in life and behavior that Calvin had stood for in Geneva and John Knox had stood for in Scotland. When they saw the men of fashion wearing long curled hair, they cut their hair short. When others dressed in silks and velvets, with ruffles and ostrich plumes, they wore plain, drab clothes made of rough material. When others drank and swore, they were sober and

157

hard-working. And they went to church, sang psalms, and read their Bibles. They made Sunday, which they called the Sabbath, a day of solemn worship when every sort of worldly distraction must stop. Early in Elizabeth's reign people who did not like their ideas gave them a name that was meant to be contemptuous. They were called the Puritans.

When James first arrived in London, some of this party put into his hands a petition for changes they were asking in the Church of England. The king called a conference at his palace at Hampton Court. But he treated the Puritans mostly with rudeness. The only thing they were interested in that he would agree to was having a new translation of the Bible. For the next seven years a company of scholars worked at it, and they produced the noble translation which has put its mark on religious life and English literature ever since. It is called the King James Version—because the translators dedicated it to him as the king.

It was during the reign of James that the religion of the Reformation was first brought to America. Roman Catholic missionaries had come earlier—the Jesuits in South America and Mexico, who began the work among the Indians that later spread to the north and produced the beautiful old Spanish mission churches, with their towers and bells, which still stand in California and New Mexico. But now the English were trying to win the North American continent instead of leaving it to either the Spanish or the French. Part of the Atlantic coast already visited by English voyagers had been named Virginia in honor of Elizabeth the virgin queen. Now a company was organized to send a colony there, with the idea of finding riches but also to carry to the new land English ways and English worship. So in 1607 three little ships crossed the ocean and landed at the mouth of a river in Virginia. They named the river the James, and their first settlement Jamestown, after the name of the king.

Among the colonists was Robert Hunt, a clergyman of the Church of England. On the first Sunday a sail was spread between two trees to form a covering over a Communion table made from logs, and Robert Hunt celebrated the Communion according to the *Book of Common Prayer*.

But in England itself were men and women who were more and more discontented with the Church's rule. They wanted to be let alone to worship in their own way. They met in one another's houses to read the Bible and to interpret it for themselves. They were strict in their behavior, and they were outraged when the king and the bishops put out what was called *The Book of Sports*. This said that people should be allowed their play on Sunday, such as Maypoles, dancing, and bowling on the greens. The Puritans thought this was a wicked breaking of the commandment that said, "Remember the sabbath day, to keep it holy." The law said that they had to worship in the regular parish churches, but they began to meet instead in their own groups. So they became known as the Independents and the Separatists.

Around the little village of Scrooby in central England some of the Independents were arrested and punished. They made up their minds to leave England altogether. With great difficulty and risk they managed to make their way by ship to Holland.

There they could worship as they pleased. But they were not satisfied. They and their children would be absorbed before long into the Dutch people. They wanted to build a church and a society on their own ground. So they hired a ship that would take most of them back to the coast of England. There at Plymouth they were met by friends who wanted to join their venture. As quietly as they could, they made arrangement for another ship that would take them across the Atlantic. On September 6, 1620, the "Mayflower" set sail. Two months later, driven by storms far north of the coast of Virginia it was headed for, the crowded and battered ship came in sight of what is now called Cape Cod. With winter drawing near, the little company of men and women and children landed on the barren shore; and in December they chose their place to settle and called it by the name of the English port town they had sailed from—Plymouth.

William Bradford, elected governor of the colony, described in his *History of Plymouth Plantation* the prospect the would-be settlers faced—a prospect such as that faced by the earlier colonists at Jamestown, but even more bleak because of the time of year when they arrived.

Being thus past the vast ocean . . . , they had now no friends to welcome them, nor inns to entertain or refresh their weatherbeaten bodies, no houses or much less towns to repair to, to seek for succor. . . . And for the season, it was winter, and they that know the winters of that country know them to be sharp and violent and subject to cruel and fierce storms, dangerous to travel to known places, much more to search an unknown coast. . . . If they look behind them, there was the mighty ocean which they had passed and was now as main bar and gulf to separate them from all the civil parts of the world.

By the next spring forty-four of the hundred who had landed in December were dead and their bodies laid in the new graves dug on Burial Hill. But the settlement, like that at Jamestown, held on. A few more ships came from England to the Plymouth colony; and nine years later a larger group landed not far north of them, to found the town of Boston, which was to grow into the colony of Massachusetts.

Both at Plymouth and at Boston and in the towns that grew up near Boston, such as Salem, the colonists were determined to regulate all their society and its government according to the religious convictions that had made them leave their homes in England. They followed and meant to enforce the strict standards of behavior that the Puritans had been fighting for all through the reign of King James. They thought that the Church of England had grown worldly and careless, and they meant to get away from its control. Especially they would have no bishops. Each congregation should elect its own minister and control its own affairs. Thus the churches that grew up in New England had the name of Congregational. In the minds of the colonists they now had religious freedom.

But though they were free from what they had not liked in England, they had no idea of letting every individual be free to think and act as he by himself might prefer. They had a strict conscience as to what they believed that the truth of God required. They enacted laws for belief and worship as fixed and full of punishments as the laws had been in England. The difference was that these were rules set up by the majority in the colony and not by king or bishop. The rules were *their* choice and not somebody else's.

But real religious freedom meant more than that, and someone was to realize it. Presently a man came to the colony of Massachusetts who did. This was the young Roger Williams. He landed in Boston in 1631. In England he had belonged to the strict Puritan party, and he was the sort of person who would fight for his convictions no matter what might happen. From Boston he went to Salem as assistant pastor in the Salem church and then to Plymouth for two years there. After that, back to Salem, and by this time the authorities in Boston decided that the colony must not put up with the ideas that he was teaching. Roger Williams had dared to say that the colony had no right to the lands that King James had granted to it. The land had belonged to the Indians, he said, and still belonged to them unless they sold it. Moreover, he said that no magistrate or anybody else ought to control any man's conscience or try to judge what he must or must not believe.

The general court of the colony declared these to be "dangerous opinions." It ordered Roger Williams to come before it, and it condemned him to leave the colony within six weeks. When the court heard a little later that Roger Williams was having people in his house and that "he preached to them, even of such points as he had been censured for," it sent out officers to arrest him. The only way he escaped arrest was by flight into the Indian country, where—as he told of it—"for fourteen weeks, in a bitter winter season, I was sorely tossed and knew not what bread or bed did mean."

Already, while he was in Plymouth, Williams had visited in the Indians' lodges and had learned their language. Now with a few companions he made his way out of the reach of the Massachusetts colony, and at the head of a great salt bay he bought land from the Narraganset tribe. There he established his first settlement and named it Providence. Out of it was to grow the colony of Rhode Island.

Other settlers followed from Massachusetts. Among them was

a Baptist preacher, and Roger Williams was rebaptized. The Baptist Church won many followers in Rhode Island, but Roger Williams later preferred to call himself a "Seeker," or Independent. And he made the colony of Rhode Island a "shelter for persons distressed in conscience." There as in no other colony of New England every person was free in the matter of religion to follow his own conviction.

Meanwhile in England the reign of James I came to its end. In 1625 he died and was succeeded by his son, Charles I. Charles was a man whose personal life everyone could admire, but he had the proud and dangerous idea that a king had a divine right to rule. He tried to govern without the English Parliament, and resistance spread among the people. The Puritans especially turned against him because he agreed with his archbishop, William Laud. Laud was determined to force everyone in England and in Scotland to worship according to the Church's rule. In Edinburgh, when the Prayer Book was used as Laud had ordered, a woman in the Scottish congregation threw a stool at the preacher's head.

Worse than that was to happen in England. Anger against the archbishop grew so great that the king could not protect him. Laud was tried, condemned, and executed. Civil war broke out against the king himself. An army from Scotland joined with an army of the English Puritans. The king's forces were defeated, and the king himself was brought to trial on the charge of treason against the people. He was condemned, led from his palace to a scaffold in Whitehall, London, and his head cut off.

Then for eleven years there was no king in England. The country was ruled by Parliament, with Oliver Cromwell, the general of the Puritan army, as Lord Protector. All the rules for the Church which Archbishop Laud and King Charles had set up were done away with. The Church in England now should be Presbyterian, like that in Scotland. A Puritan assembly drew up the Westminster Confession, which was a statement of faith like the teachings of Calvin, and the Westminster Catechism, which all good Presbyterians were supposed to learn.

Before long, however, England grew tired of the Puritan Parliament. Not only those who had been loyal to Charles I but others also were ready to have a king again. The son of Charles I, who had been an exile in France, returned and was crowned in London as Charles the Second.

Now the laws concerning the Church and how people must worship in it went back about to what they had been in the time of Archbishop Laud. But all the same there were still people who were not going to obey.

Some of the English Separatists who had gone to Holland had met there the Mennonites, who were Anabaptists. Their ideas of the freedom of every individual's conscience, no rule by the state over any man's conscience, and baptism only for believers were brought to England. In England the men and women of this persuasion came to be called by a shorter name—not Anabaptists, but Baptists.

The most famous among them was John Bunyan. He was a tinker's son, but he had learned to read and write. As a young man he was a soldier in the Puritan army that had fought against the king. For a long while he was in great distress of mind and soul because he thought he was a hopeless sinner. He joined a Baptist congregation in Bedfordshire, where he lived. Then presently he began to preach.

He had no license, and by the rules of the Church he had no business to be preaching. As soon as Charles II became king, Bunyan was arrested and put in Bedford jail. He was married, and he had four children. One of them, for whom his love was tenderest, was his little daughter who was blind. It tore his heart to think that with him in jail his wife and children might have to beg to keep alive. The magistrates mocked his belief that he was called to preach. They said that what he was meant for was mending kettles. If he would promise to stop preaching, they would let him go. If not, he should stay in jail and perhaps be hanged. But Bunyan answered, "If you let me out today, I will preach again tomorrow."

Bedford jail was a wretched, filthy place. Bunyan was kept there for most of twelve years. His jailers could not dream that while they were stopping him from preaching, he would be doing something that would move more people than almost any preacher who has ever lived. He wrote *Pilgrim's Progress*. Later it was printed, and tens of thousands of copies went out everywhere. It had in it the tremendous message of the Bible for souls that wanted to be saved, and it was put into an exciting story. It was written in language that the simplest people could understand. Not only Baptists but Christian people of every name and rank would bless John Bunyan.

Besides the Baptists there was another group of people in England that ran afoul of the law, not only under the first and second King Charles, but also under the government by Parliament in between. These were the Society of Friends, who were also called the Quakers.

They were the followers of George Fox, and George Fox seemed to people of orderly habits to go clear beyond the bounds of everything that was respectable. He said that all church buildings were nothing but vain "steeple houses." He said that a man was not fit to be a minister just because he had studied at Oxford or Cambridge. There ought not to be any regular ministers anyhow. Christian believers should meet together and wait for the Spirit to move them. Then whoever were moved by the Spirit, women as well as men, let them speak and testify. There should be no baptism or Communion service, for they were only empty signs, said Fox. Everything depended on what he called the "inner light." None could be considered "true believers except such as were born of God and had passed from death unto life."

Fox had no respect for magistrates or for courts. He would not take off his hat anywhere or to anybody. Once when he went into a church where the minister was preaching about the Bible, he stood up and shouted out that the church where they were gathered was nothing but an idol; and as to what the preacher was saying, he ought to know that the Bible could not be understood except by those who had the divine light within themselves. Another time he walked barefoot through one of the cathedral towns on market day, crying out, "Woe to the bloody city of Lichfield!"

Of course he was arrested, for the authorities thought he was no better than a wild man. He was in jail again and again, and all his followers were savagely treated. But Fox said, "I have never feared death nor suffering." Even the officers who arrested him were bound to say, "He is as stiff as a tree, and as pure as a bell." And although at first the Quakers roused hostility every-where by what seemed their stubborn ways and by different dress, they were men and women of courage and of a pure love for God. They would swear no oath. They would not take part in any war. Their conscience made them just and peaceable.

Religion as the Quakers preached and practiced it won con-verts not only among the plain people but also among some who held high rank. One of these men of privilege who became a Quaker was William Penn, the son of Sir William Penn, admiral in the British navy. As a boy William Penn had had a sudden religious experience, in which he was "surprised with an inward comfort," during which he was overcome with a great sense of the reality of God and a conviction "that the soul of man was capable of enjoying communication with Him." As a young man at Oxford, William Penn began to rebel against what he thought was the lifeless worship in the Church of England services. In spite of his father's great displeasure he became a Quaker preacher; and when Quaker meetinghouses were closed by the authorities, he preached to people in the streets. Fre-quently he was arrested for "breach of the peace" and "unlawful assembly," and put in prison—in Ireland, in the Tower of London, and in other English jails. But he kept on declaring that every man's conscience must be free. Powerful influence which he and his family had in the court of Charles II prevented such long imprisonments for him as those to which John Bunyan had been condemned. However often he was in jail, he got out again. And what he preached about his religious faith and what he wrote in a flood of pamphlets won respect even from those who at first had no use for his ideas.

Moreover, King Charles liked him. The king knew that Penn

was interested in America, and in 1681 he made him a grant of a great tract of land west of the Delaware River. Penn founded a colony there which he wanted to name Sylvania, but King Charles insisted that Penn's own name should be linked with it. So it became Pennsylvania.

In the new colony Penn provided that all men should have freedom in religion, such as Roger Williams had already established in Rhode Island. Also his Quaker principles showed in the kind of government he established, which was meant to give justice and security to all the people. The town that was to grow into the chief city of the colony was named Philadelphia, which means the City of Brotherly Love. Unlike what happened in most of the other colonies, he tried to deal fairly with the Indians and to treat them not as enemies but as friends. Therefore the western frontiers of Pennsylvania were quiet when other colonies were continually in danger from the arrows and tomahawks of Indians who might come bursting from the woods.

On Manhattan Island, at the mouth of the Hudson River, the Dutch had established at the beginning of the seventeenth century the log fort and the few houses of their settlement of New Amsterdam (afterward to become New York). With the Dutch pioneers there came the Reformed Church—the form of Calvinism which had fought for its life in Holland a half century earlier in the heroic struggle by which the Low Countries won their independence from the Roman Catholic Philip II of Spain.

Soon after the Dutch had founded New Amsterdam, German Lutherans followed as settlers in the Hudson valley. Other Lutherans, from Sweden, built churches in Wilmington, Delaware, and in Philadelphia; and many thousands more from the Lutheran countries of Europe came into Pennsylvania. Further organization of Lutheran churches and the development of Lutheran worship in all the colonies were inspired by the great pastor and preacher Henry Melchior Muhlenberg, who came from Germany in 1742; and from that time on Lutheranism became one of the powerful religious influences in the new world, as it had already been in Europe.

CHAPTER 29

THE GOSPEL COMES
TO THE COMMON PEOPLE

OR A long time men had had to hold their religious faith at the cost of risk and danger. They might be imprisoned and even put to death for not believing as those who were in power said they must. Whole countries were torn with religious conflict. In England there was the rebellion against Charles I, at the end of which not only an archbishop but also the king himself had been beheaded. At that same time there went on in the center of Europe the dreadful struggle, with its ruinous plundering and killing, that was called the Thirty Years' War. Whether they were right or wrong, men could be fearfully in earnest.

At long last, and gradually, there came a change. Men in authority stopped believing that it was their duty to make all men think alike. Religious wars were coming to an end. So far, so good. As men's passions cooled, there was less religious conflict. But what if there was less religious conviction too?

For a while it looked as though that was happening. With many people, what religion they had was comfortable and easy-going. In Europe in the 1700's men were living in what they liked to call the Age of Enlightenment. There was elegant life and much learning, and it began to be thought that the world could get on very well as it was. It was admitted that God had made the world, but it was said that having made it he had left it like a wound-up clock to run itself. Men's minds were so smoothly ordered that all they had to do now was to live according to reason. Nobody needed to bother about his sins or about salvation either.

At least that is what the men at the top were thinking. The great mass of people were not thinking much of anything, for they were too poor and ignorant. There needed to be churches that would go out and bring the love of God to those who had never heard of it. But mostly the churches were not doing that. They were not doing that in Roman Catholic France, where the dull anger of the people was to break out presently into the French Revolution. They were not doing that in other countries of Europe. And they were not doing it in Protestant England either.

Many of the clergy were lazy and some of them of doubtful morals. Even among the best of them there was often an easy-going worldliness. They might be kindly men as long as they were comfortable, but they did not go out of their way to find the people who needed them most. The Rev. James Woodforde, whose ministry was in country parishes of the Church of England in the late 1700's, kept a diary. In his diary he noted down the services he conducted in church, and sometimes he told the text of a sermon. But he seldom gave any sign that his heart was in preaching the gospel or that he thought people needed to hear it. But he had a great deal to say in his diary of what he ate for breakfast, dinner, and supper, of the inns he slept in, the fine houses where he visited, the wines he drank, and his pleasures generally. One day he wrote: "I made all my Company quite merry. We drank 8 bottles of Port, one bottle of Madeira, besides Arrac Punch, Beer and Cyder. I carried on my drinking exceedingly well indeed."

Meanwhile there was not much effort to make the church reach out to all the people. Most of the clergy just let things drift along. If the church doors were open on Sunday and the services read, that was all they thought they had to concern themselves about. Out in the village there might be sodden poverty and wretchedness, drunken men and miserable women; but what else could you expect of the "lower classes"? If they had come to church and had wanted to be respectable, they would have been different. But if they wanted to be as they were, what could anybody do about it? That is what too many well-fed parsons of the Church of England in that time were inclined to say.

Then something different happened.

Near the city of Bristol, first in the street and then in an open field outside, a man was preaching. This man also was a clergyman of the Church of England, who said that before this he would "have thought the saving of souls almost a sin, if it had not been in a church." But now to three thousand people who gathered about him he was preaching from the text, "The Spirit of the Lord is upon me, because he hath anointed me to preach the gospel to the poor; he hath sent me to heal the brokenhearted, to preach deliverance to the captives, and recovering of sight to the blind, to set at liberty them that are bruised, to preach the acceptable year of the Lord." On the man's face was the light of a great conviction. In his voice was a passion of pity and appeal. The crowd around him was not made up of those who would be at the parish church in their Sunday clothes. Here were the poor and grimy people: dirty-faced men from the coalpits, rough drivers from their carts, plowboys from the fields, women from the alleys of the town. To all of them he was pouring out his message of the love of God—and the call of God to repent and to let their whole lives be converted.

The man was John Wesley, who did more for the England of his lifetime than statesmen and kings could do.

He was born in 1703 in an English rectory, the fifteenth child of Samuel and Susannah Wesley. When he was old enough to enter Oxford University, he had gained from his mother's training a devotion to the Church. In college he was the head of a little group who were bent on making their religion real. They met in Wesley's rooms on Sunday evenings, then presently somewhere every evening. They studied the New Testament, went to Communion, and tried to examine their lives in the light of the gospel.

When he had been ordained a clergyman, Wesley went about his duties faithfully, influenced—as many others were—by the consecrated Cambridge scholar William Law and his book *A Serious Call to a Devout and Holy Life*. With his brother Charles, John Wesley sailed for America, hoping to be a missionary to the Indians. This did not work out, and he returned to London.

He was not happy, though he had tried to be faithful to his work. Something was lacking. He wanted to serve God, but he did not have the grace and power from God he needed.

Then in London on one particular evening all life changed for him. He went to a meeting of some Christians from Moravia, followers of John Huss. They were reading from what Martin Luther had written on the apostle Paul's letter to the Romans, about how a man is changed not by what he can do himself but by what is already done for him by the love of Christ. Just as it had been with Luther, so now suddenly John Wesley "felt [his] heart strangely warmed." From that moment he had a power to live by and a gospel that he could preach with all his soul and strength.

Wesley wanted to preach it in the regular pulpits of the Church of England. But the rectors and vicars of sleepy old parishes thought he would make a disturbance. Wesley's preaching would excite the common people, and they did not want what they thought would be the drunken and dirty ragtag and bobtail crowd coming into their pews. They would not invite Wesley. One time when Wesley was on his way to a church where he thought he would be allowed to preach, he received a note, "Our minister, having been informed you are beside yourself, does not care you should preach in any of his churches."

Another clergyman of the Church, George Whitefield, had begun to preach outdoors. Wesley was following his example. It was dangerous business. He was jeered at and sometimes howled down. In the little towns of England were some so sunk in drunkenness and crime that the last person they wanted to look at was a preacher. They threw mud and filth at Wesley. Once a club flung at him nearly hit his head. But he kept on. Crowds grew, and they began to listen. Even the hoodlums changed. At one place where Wesley was preaching, the leader of a gang who were about to pull Wesley off his platform suddenly was so moved by Wesley's courage that he sprang up in front of him. "I'll stand by you," he shouted; and he dared anyone in the crowd to touch him.

All over England now there began to be conversions. "I have

seen very many persons changed in a moment," Wesley wrote
in his journal, "from the spirit of fear, horror, despair, to the
spirit of love, joy and peace, and from sinful desire, till then
reigning over them, to a pure desire of doing the will of God."

And Wesley did not stop with preaching. He, and his brother
Charles even more, wrote hymns that were sung all over England
—and are in nearly every Christian hymnbook now. These are
the first lines of some of the most beautiful and best-loved ones:

> Hark! the herald angels sing,
> "Glory to the newborn King."

> Come, Thou long-expected Jesus,
> Born to set Thy people free.

> Christ the Lord is risen today, . . .
> Sons of men and angels say.

> Lo, He comes with clouds descending,
> Once for our salvation slain.

> Love divine, all loves excelling,
> Joy of heaven, to earth come down.

> Jesus, Lover of my soul,
> Let me to Thy bosom fly.

> Jesus, Thy boundless love to me
> No thought can reach, no tongue declare.

> Soldiers of Christ, arise,
> And put your armor on.

John Wesley organized his converts into little groups to help
and encourage one another. He did not leave their Christian life
to chance. He gave his people ways and methods for prayer
and for testimony and for work. So his societies began to be
called the Methodists.

He was nearly eighty-eight years old when he died. He had
gone through England, Scotland, Wales, and Ireland, preaching
wherever people were—in fields, in market places, in jails. He

went on horseback, reading a book as he rode. It was figured that in his lifetime he had ridden more than 200,000 miles. No one could count how many he had preached to, and the number of those whose hearts he had touched and changed could be known only to God.

While this spiritual awakening was developing in England, a new influence was appearing in America.

In most of the colonies the first settlers who came were men who were seeking the right to worship in the way they chose. Their morals were high and their convictions strong. But after them came others who were more interested in something else. They wanted a chance to make a better living than they could hope for in the little villages and the crowded old cities of England. The tales that came back about the great new land made them think that everybody could have a new start there. So they began to get passage on ships that were sailing west, some of them with a little money of their own, some of them hired out in advance as servants to the colonists. Some were of sturdy English stock that knew how to work and also how to fight. Some were shiftless. And many of them were the sort of people John Wesley had been preaching to in England. They had good hearts if anyone could get at them, but they were rough and uneducated, more inclined to get drunk and gamble and carouse than to go to church. Something more startling than the regular pulpit preaching was needed to get hold of them.

And as time went on, the same might be true of some of the respectable church people who thought they were as good as they needed to be, but actually had lost the fire their fathers had.

Then there began what was called the Great Awakening. In Massachusetts in the town of Northampton a young Congregational minister named Jonathan Edwards was preaching. In his manner of preaching he did not seem to be any great orator, but he had a powerful mind; and—what was more—he had a burning conviction. He looked at the people who were careless and indifferent, and one Sunday in July, 1741, he preached a sermon on the text "Their foot shall slide in due time." The subject and title of that sermon was "Sinners in the Hands of an Angry God."

Jonathan Edwards did not always preach on a subject so stern and terrible as that. At other times he preached on the love and peace of God that could be in people's hearts. But this time he had the passionate purpose to make loose-living people stop and see the danger to their souls. One of those who heard him wrote that they were "deeply impressed and bowed down, with an awful conviction of their sin and danger. There was such a breathing of distress and weeping, that the preacher was obliged to speak to the people and desire silence, that he might be heard." And it was said that, as he preached, some of the congregation cried out and caught hold of the backs of the pews in front of them as though to keep from sliding straight down to hell.

About that same time the great evangelist, George Whitefield, who had started John Wesley to preaching outdoors in England, came to America. For four years he went through the colonies, exhorting such crowds as few had ever seen. He had an amazing voice, so strong and clear that it was said that he could make twenty thousand people hear him in an open field. The roads would be like clouds of dust for miles around the place where one of his meetings was to be held, as men on horseback and families in wagons came from villages and farms to hear him. And Whitefield poured out all his soul and strength. When John Wesley saw him later, he said that "he seemed to be an old man, being fairly worn out in his Master's service, though he had hardly seen fifty years." But when Whitefield's friends advised him to take some rest, he replied: "I would rather *wear* out than *rust* out."

CHAPTER 30

WHEN THE CHURCH SAW
THE WHOLE WORLD'S NEED

OMETHING ELSE happened in the churches that could be called a Great Enlightenment. It was a new beginning in missionary work.

Men like George Whitefield who came from England to America might be thought of as missionaries in the fact that they were sent out to preach the gospel away from home. Also there were societies of the Church of England that sent out clergymen to Virginia and other colonies. But their work—except for a few who like the devoted John Eliot in Massachusetts tried to reach the Indians—was among their own English-speaking people in their own lands. What about all the millions of people of many races and languages in other countries of the earth? Why should not the gospel that told of Jesus and of the love of God in him be carried to those who had never heard it?

That was what some greathearted men in other centuries had asked, and they went out themselves to be the answer. Patrick had gone to Ireland, Columba to Scotland, and Boniface to Germany when the people in those countries were all pagans. When the Roman Catholic Church woke to new life after the Reformation, Jesuit priests had gone out heroically to India, Japan, and China, and among the red Indian tribes of the new world.

Among Protestants the first to think of sending out missionaries to people outside the Christian lands were the Moravian Brethren. They were descended from the early followers of John Huss, the heroic reformer who was burned at the stake in 1415. The Brethren had been fiercely persecuted, and in the dreadful religious struggles that began in 1618 and continued as the Thirty Years' War they were almost exterminated. Only a few, who were called the "Hidden Seed," survived in Moravia. When new per-

176

secutions broke out, some of them escaped to Germany. There they found refuge on the Saxon estates of Count Zinzendorf, a devoted Lutheran; and they built their town of Herrnhut. It was in a worship service of some of the Brethren who had gone to England that John Wesley had his great new experience of conversion. Some of those same Brethren had been in the new American colonies of Georgia and Carolina; and others went out to preach the gospel in Greenland, in Labrador, in the Danish West Indies, and in part of South America.

Now it was time that someone in England should follow their example. In Northamptonshire there was a young Baptist preacher named William Carey. He had to do some other work in order to earn enough to live, so he sat at a bench cobbling shoes. The little shop where he worked was narrow, but his thoughts were as wide as the world. He kept a map in front of him; and as he looked at it, he thought of peoples around the earth to whom the gospel had not been taken. Somebody must take it. Perhaps God meant that the somebody should be William Carey, said William Carey to himself.

On May 31, 1792, he went to a meeting of Baptist preachers at Nottingham. He had been chosen to give the sermon that day. He stood up and spoke on the text from the book of the prophet Isaiah, "Lengthen thy cords, and strengthen thy stakes." Isaiah was thinking of the religion of his people as like a tent. To lengthen its cords meant to spread it wide, but a tent can safely be spread wider only when its stakes are driven deeper into the ground. That is the way it ought to be with the Church, William Carey said. Let it reach out further, and at the same time it can be more sure and strong. "Attempt great things for God; expect great things from God." This was the message he brought that day.

Of course there were some who shook their heads. How could a little group of plain people in England be expected to carry the gospel across the world? If God wanted people off there to be Christians, he would see to it himself.

Yes, he may see to it, and see to it through using *me*, said William Carey and a few who agreed with him. Most of those who

had heard Carey were not much moved. But after a time twelve persons met together in the back parlor of a widow's house in the little town of Kettering. They took up a collection among themselves that added up to twelve pounds, two shillings, and six-pence. That was all they had. But that with faith in God was enough to be the beginning of the movement that would send missionaries of the gospel across the world.

Carey had read about the voyages of the famous Captain Cook, who a few years earlier had been the first man to explore the islands in the vast South Seas. Carey's first desire was to carry the gospel there; but that was not possible, and the chance came to sail instead for India. For fourteen months after he had left on the long, slow voyage of fifteen thousand miles, no word came back from Carey to the little company praying for him at home.

And when at last a letter did come, it hardly seemed encourag-ing. The East India Company, which controlled all the ports of India, refused to allow Carey to land. He had to go to a nearby Portuguese settlement and later to the Danish colony of Seram-pore. It was to take him many years before he won his first Indian convert.

But Carey's faith never failed. "I have God, and his word is sure," he wrote. "God's cause will triumph, and I shall come out of all trials as gold purified by fire."

He established not only a church and a school but also the first printing press in India. With immense industry he trans-lated the Bible into the various languages and dialects of India, and twenty thousand copies of it were sent out from his press in Serampore. As his influence grew, he was able to persuade the British governors of India to put an end to the ancient and cruel practice of suttee, the custom that when a man died, his widow must be burned with him on his funeral pyre. Carey never ceased his work nor came home again; and when he died in 1834 his mission in northern India had grown to thirty stations with sixty-three Europeans and Indians serving in them.

Meanwhile Carey's example had kindled new devotion among Christians who formerly had had no missionary fire.

Three years after Carey's sermon on "Attempt great things

for God; expect great things from God" leaders of different churches formed the London Missionary Society. In the year following, 1796, money had been raised to buy and equip the ship "Duff." Twenty-nine persons had volunteered to go as missionaries to Tahiti and to the other islands in the far South Seas where Carey at first had wanted to go. And when the "Duff" slipped its moorings at the London docks and headed down the river toward the sea, it was said that there was a "vast multitude beholding," and that there had been no other vessel "in which so many thousands of Christians embarked their hopes and followed with their prayers."

The missionary spirit spread to America. In Williamstown, Massachusetts, and at Andover a little company of men pledged themselves to carry the gospel wherever God's spirit might call them to go. Like Carey they started for India. But the one among them who was to become most famous, Adoniram Judson, came instead into Burma. There was hardly any sort of hardship that he did not face. For two years he had to endure heat, hunger, brutal treatment, and fever in filthy prisons, most of the time in chains. When he was asked what he thought was the prospect for his work, he answered, "Wait twenty years and then look this way again. It is as bright as the promises."

Whoever did look that way again at Judson's work would have seen before long the Bible translated into the Burman language and whole tribes, especially the Karens, won to Christianity. And anyone who reads *Burma Surgeon,* by the medical missionary Gordon Seagrave, will have a picture of what the Christian influence that Adoniram Judson started has blossomed into.

The same London Missionary Society that sent out the men and women on the "Duff" to the South Seas sent another missionary to a harder task. This was Robert Morrison, and the field he was to try to enter was the vast empire of China. An agent of the shipping company asked him scornfully, "So then, Mr. Morrison, you really expect to make an impression on the Chinese people?" "No, sir," he answered, "but I expect God will."

All he could do was to wait on the Portuguese island of Macao, off the China coast, where he translated the Bible into Chinese.

Then he got as far as the port city of Canton, but he was allowed no farther. In seven years he made only one Chinese convert. It looked as though the shipping agent had been right in his scornful idea that no Christian missionary would ever accomplish anything in China.

But the truth was different. Christian missionaries by the hundreds did finally win their way into China: ministers, teachers, doctors, nurses. Not only have they drawn tens of thousands of Chinese into Christian congregations; they have developed Chinese leaders who can take the Church in China into their own hands. So also it has been in Japan, in India, in the East Indies, and elsewhere in the Orient. When a great Christian assembly met in Madras in 1938, the roll of representatives there from the "younger churches" showed that the Christian Church was established in eleven Asian countries.

So the last century and a half has seen Christianity spread more widely in the world that it was ever spread before. Missions and missionaries have had their mistakes, their weaknesses, and sometimes their failures. But in their purpose and their spirit they have represented the outreaching love of Christ.

And besides the average men and women who will be remembered only by those who knew them best, there have been also the great figures who will never be forgotten. Such have been David Livingstone, who gave his life to destroy the African slave trade; the young doctor Wilfred Grenfell, who left London to devote himself completely to the needs of the deep-sea fishermen on the icy coasts of Labrador; and Albert Schweitzer, one of the world's great scholars and musicians, who left the fame he might have had at home to build his hospital for the black tribes at Lambaréné, on the African equator.

At the middle of the twentieth century the Christian Church in many countries was cut off from the rest of the world. In China, in Russia, and in some of the smaller states under Russian control it may be persecuted. But Christianity has endured persecution before. And the words of William Carey still are true: "God's cause will triumph, and I shall come out of all trials as gold purified by fire."

CHAPTER 31

THE MEANING
OF MISSIONS REDISCOVERED

I N EVEN the countries from which the great missionary movements had gone out, there were many people who had only indifferent ideas about them. They took it for granted that some persons would want to go out to preach Christianity in out-of-the-way places, but they did not know why. It might not occur to the average churchgoer in America that the results of Christian missions might be of exceeding importance to him.

But through the World War that began in 1939 many have had a new lesson, and this is the story of how that happened.

In the immense spaces of the Pacific Ocean north of Australia there lies a chain of islands that through many centuries no man from Europe or America had ever seen. In 1567, seventy-five years after the voyage of Columbus, a Spanish sea captain named Mendaña set out across the Pacific from Peru. Nearly four thousand miles he sailed; and then one day he caught sight of great mountains rising from the sea, with deep lagoons where ships could anchor, and beyond these rivers and forests and fertile valleys full of tropical fruit. It all seemed so wonderful to Mendaña that he thought of the richest person he had ever read about, King Solomon; and he named his discovery the Solomon Islands.

But the natives on the islands were not as agreeable as their islands. They were naked savages who fought among themselves on land and raided along the coasts in their war canoes. They cut off the heads of enemies they had killed, and hung them up as trophies in their huts. Also they were cannibals. It was not strange, then, that Mendaña did not linger. And after his discovery the Solomon Islands were forgotten for nearly three hundred years.

Then they began to be visited by a kind of white men more

evil than the dark-skinned natives. Trading ships anchored off
the islands, and the natives were enticed on board with promises
of presents. When the white men had got some of them to go
below deck, they shut the hatches, hauled up the anchor, and
sailed off with their captives to sell them into slavery. So it was
no wonder that the islanders began to fear and hate the sight of
any white man's face. If a missionary should come, they would
not know him from a trader. And they would not stop to find
out.

In 1845 the first missionaries did land in the Solomons, a little
band of heroic Roman Catholic priests. Their leader was murdered on the first day. Within a year three more had been killed
and eaten in cannibal feasts. Later all the rest were killed or died
of fever.

But the missionary purpose, once the love of Christ had started
it, could not be discouraged. It was the Church of England that
next dared to carry the gospel among the island savages. Seven
years after the Roman Catholic mission had failed, Bishop Selwyn
of New Zealand began to cruise among the other islands. Inspired by him, a brilliant young graduate of Oxford, John Coleridge Patteson, came out from England to join him. After a time
Patteson was made bishop of Melanesia, the larger group of islands of which the Solomons were a part. On his little schooner,
the "Southern Cross," he went from island to island, landing at
risk of his life. On one island, when he was taken into the chief's
council hut, he saw on the ridgepole twenty-eight human skulls.
Two of them had been nailed there such a little while before
that they had not begun to be darkened like the others by the
smoke of the council fire.

There in those surroundings, where head-hunting and can-
nibalism and witchcraft still prevailed, John Coleridge Patteson
lived and worked. People who had been raw savages began to
trust him. Some of the young men were converted. And not only
that. They were trained by the bishop to be evangelists and
teachers of a new way of life to their own people.

Then one day a canoe was found floating on the sea. In it was
the body of Bishop Patteson, pierced by five great wounds. He

had landed on an island where he was not known. The natives had mistaken him for a trader who had carried off five of their people. So they had taken what they thought at first was their revenge. But in Bishop Patteson's hand was a palm branch and on his breast another palm as a sign that those who killed him had found out their mistake and honored him as best they could.

It was not the wounds but the palm of victory that would tell the fullest story about the mission's work. The Church of England mission grew. Other missionaries came to the islands, especially Methodists and Lutherans.

Nearly a hundred years went by. Now in the South Pacific there was war. The Japanese navy steamed down through all that sea, landed troops upon the islands, and took possession of them. Then came an American and Australian fleet to try to take the islands from the Japanese. To the young American and Australian sailors, soldiers, and airmen the beaches on which they landed or the jungles on which they looked down seemed to hold nothing but hidden danger. They knew the Japanese were there. If any others were in those jungles, they supposed they would be savages, more dangerous than any Japanese.

What happened? Something so astonishing that it seemed to many of these American and Australian boys as though they had dropped into a land of miracles. Black men on the islands who they thought were savages and heathen turned out to be better Christians than they themselves might be. Those same men had been savages, and they were the descendants of the head-hunters and the cannibals who had killed the first missionaries that came to the South Seas. But now they were friends and rescuers. Airmen shot down at sea and making their way to shore were picked up and hidden from the Japanese. Wounded men were carried into the hills and nursed. One American private wrote home, "I wish I could say that the American people could be half the Christians that these natives are. Believe me, they aren't in the least backward in owning up to being Christians. They're proud to be one."

On the island of Guadalcanal, where sixteen hundred American men who died there are buried, four thousand of the islanders built a chapel out of the native wood, with a bell tower and a cross. On the chapel they carved these words:

> This Is the House of God
> This Is None Other than the Gate of Heaven

And when it was dedicated, a Christian named Jason, the head of the workers, said in his broken English, "Now we give this church to you. But this church no belong to you and me. This church belong to God. And we ask God to bless us all."

CHAPTER 32

CHRISTIAN CHURCHES
IN THE UNITED STATES

FTER THE Revolutionary War, when the American colonies became the United States, it was determined that the government should never have control over anyone's religion. Every man should be free to follow his own conscience and to worship in the church he should choose, or not to worship.

There had been a time when Christian people thought of themselves as belonging to the Church and not to different churches. For many centuries in Europe that had been true. Then corruptions that had crept into the Church had made men like Wycliffe and John Huss and Martin Luther lift up their protests in the name of the gospel that was being forgotten. Their purpose was to purify the Church and not to split it. But when the popes and the other rulers would not listen, the great reformers had to preach the truth as they believed it to those who dared to rally round them. Thus the different churches developed out of what had been the one Church—and is meant to be the one Church in a way deeper than the difference of names. For all Christian people look to one Lord and Savior, Jesus Christ; and their right to be called Christians is according to how true they are to him. In the free land of America every church would have an equal chance to show how real is its religion.

In Massachusetts and in most of New England were the Congregationalists. In Rhode Island there were many Baptists, descended from those who had followed Roger Williams, the pioneer. In New York, when it was New Amsterdam, the church had been the Dutch Reformed; but when the English captured the colony, the Church of England also came. In and around Pennsylvania were the Quakers, and in Delaware the Lutherans. Because Lord Baltimore, to whom the colony of Maryland had been granted by King Charles I, was a Roman Catholic, many Catholics as well as Protestants had settled there; and—as hardly anywhere else in those times—the two groups lived peaceably together.

In Virginia all through the colonial period there was the same established Church of England that had been brought by the first settlers who landed in Jamestown in 1607. With the end of the Revolutionary War the link with England was broken, and there was need for a reorganization and for American bishops. The clergy in Connecticut were the first to elect a bishop, and they sent Samuel Seabury to England to be consecrated by the bishops there. But the English law, as it then read, prohibited consecrating a bishop unless he pledged allegiance to the king. So Seabury went to Scotland; and in Aberdeen in 1784 three Scottish bishops, who were not bound by English law, held the service of consecration according to the historic rites. The English law was soon modified; and in 1787 two more American bishops, William White and Samuel Provoost, were consecrated in London by the Archbishop of Canterbury. Thus provision was fully made for the establishment and continuance of the episcopate in America. Meanwhile White had been trying for several years to bring representatives together for organization, and at length in 1789 he succeeded in assembling a General Convention in his home city of Philadelphia. This body adopted a constitution for the Protestant Episcopal Church and a *Book of Common Prayer,* which embodied with only slight changes the ways of worship, the forms of ministry, and the creeds of the Church of England.

The Episcopal Church in America was affected by the same influences that moved in the mother country. In the colonies, as in England, there had been among the clergy and the people too much of the lazy worldliness that had distressed John Wesley. But before the end of Wesley's life there had arisen men in the Church of England, the Evangelicals, who preached the need of personal conversion as fervently as Wesley had preached it. Their spirit spread to America. And later another influence entered into the Episcopal Church, and in some ways into other churches also. In England in the 1830's there developed what was called the Oxford Movement. John Keble, Edward B. Pusey, John Henry Newman, and other earnest men in and around the Oxford colleges believed that what ought to be the inherited dignity and beauty of the Church's worship was being lost. They wanted Christians to recognize again the authority of ancient teachings and traditions. John Henry Newman went so far in this direction that he became a priest and later a cardinal in the Roman Catholic Church. Some of the others, as "High Churchmen," fell into the danger of looking so much to patterns of the past that they could not always appreciate new ways in which the Holy Spirit might be at work in different churches now. But in what they tried to teach there was a value that Christians of many names would begin quietly to feel: namely, that in the fellowship of the whole Church and in its proven ways there may be a wisdom deeper than one's own impatient thought.

In the far south the Huguenots, French followers of Calvin who had come to America because of persecution in their native land, joined forces with the Presbyterians, of whom large numbers had come to the middle colonies from England, Scotland, and Northern Ireland during the years when the British government was trying to enforce harsh measures against them at home. These people played a large part in developing the American principles of freedom and democracy. The Rev. John Witherspoon, who was president of their most famous school, Princeton University, served as a delegate to the Continental Congress and became the one minister to sign the Declaration of Independence. After the Revolutionary War the Presbyterians reorganized and took the leadership in a new "Awakening" that swept the country.

Though it was in Rhode Island that Baptists had first been strongest, Baptist preachers made many converts and organized congregations in other states. The Baptist belief that each congregation should conduct itself entirely by vote of the members seemed so consistent with what Americans of that time were fighting for in government that increasing numbers were attracted to it. Most of the Baptists were plain people with little wealth or social position, and they did not hesitate to urge their neighbors to join with them.

The Methodists, coming later, had no special settlement of their own. It was said of them that instead of living in a settlement, they lived in saddlebags. The preachers followed the example of John Wesley in traveling about and preaching wherever people would listen. When they settled on a customary route to follow, they called it a circuit; and thus they came to be known as circuit riders. John Wesley intended that Methodism should be simply a revival movement within the Church of England, and so it remained in Britain throughout his lifetime. But in America following the Revolutionary War it was hard to keep up this connection, and in 1784 the preachers met and established American Methodism as an independent denomination. After this they extended their circuits more widely, not only along the Atlantic coast, where most of the people were, but following the pioneers as they pushed the frontiers west; and their leader, Bishop Francis Asbury, himself rode during his career more than a quarter of a million miles.

Some of the preachers had only scanty education or special training. But they spoke the language of the people, and they made even the roughest of the pioneers remember that wherever they went, the Word of God went with them.

Among the advance guard also were the Disciples of Christ. Beginning in the early 1800's in Pennsylvania as followers of Thomas Campbell and his son Alexander Campbell, who were Presbyterians from Scotland, and believing that "division among the Christians is a horrid evil," they declared that "where the scriptures speak, we speak; where the scriptures are silent, we are silent." They held, like the Baptists, to baptism of believers by immersion; but they parted from the Baptists in other matters of doctrine and practice. They thought they could get back to Bible teaching that would be so fundamental that they would draw other Christians to them. They failed in this and became another one of the many denominations, but they have always had a zeal for Christian unity. And like the Baptists and the

Methodists they knew how to preach to the plain people and were a strong influence in evangelizing and educating the new communities into which the wagon trains of settlers from the Atlantic seaboard were pushing on.

Freedom in religion, which a few solitary men like Roger Williams and William Penn had dared to champion, had now actually become a fact in America. The Constitution of the new United States provided that there should be "no law respecting an establishment of religion, or prohibiting the free exercise thereof." No sort of church would be forbidden by the state, and no sort of church would be supported either. If Christianity was to spread, it would have to depend not upon a few officials but upon the great body of ordinary Christians and upon how much they cared. Freedom in religion had its danger in the fact that every man was at liberty to preach any belief that he might have, even though it came out of ignorance. But the great gain was that freedom gave importance to every man's convictions and could warm his impulse to express them. An individual could become a witness to the gospel, and a group of Christians could be fired by missionary purpose.

That sort of purpose was needed if the developing life of America was to have a Christian character. In the early days of the colonies nearly everybody had been a member of some church. The one great reason why many of them came to the new continent was to find a place where they could worship in ways that had not been allowed them in Europe. Then followed the years when ships brought thousands of others who were thinking not of religion but of reports they had heard that in America any man could find the big chance to get ahead. New territories were opening. At first there were only the settlements along the eastern seaboard, with the Indians and the wilderness beyond. Then the frontier was pushed to the Mississippi River, to Louisiana and Texas and New Mexico, and at length across the prairies and the Rocky Mountains to Oregon and California.

And as the country was expanding, so was the population—by increase of births here and by the pouring in of tens of thousands of immigrants from the old lands of Europe. In 1800 there were only a few more than 5,000,000 people in the United States, by 1860 there were more than 31,000,000, and the rate of increase rose rapidly after that. What would life be like out in the cabins where the forests were being cleared, on the lonely farms and ranches, in the mining camps and in the new towns that were springing up everywhere? It might turn into a rough and brawling paganism with religion left behind.

It took a vigorous kind of Christianity to give the right answer, and on the whole the answer did not fail. The people of the expanding country were not left to their own loneliness, and they were not left either to the evil forces that were always ready to follow them: the saloons, the gambling joints, the dance halls with their low seductions. The preachers and pastors followed the frontier. Long before there were church buildings, they preached wherever people could be got together. Often the message of the gospel might be given by men who had no organization anywhere to back them up—men who might not be ordained, who worked their farms on weekdays and preached somewhere on Sundays. Then missionary societies and Bible societies and societies to establish Sunday schools developed. Churches were built, and schools and hospitals and colleges. Before long there were few communities that did not have in their midst the continual reminders of a Christian way of life.

In 1800 only one person out of every nine or ten was a member of a church. By 1850 there were fifteen or sixteen to each hundred and by 1900 nearly forty. In 1950 out of every hundred of the whole population fifty-seven were at least professed members of a Christian church.

During colonial times and when the United States became an independent nation, except in Maryland there were hardly any Roman Catholics. Beginning about 1850 and in the fifty or sixty years after that hundreds of thousands came from Ireland and from other Roman Catholic countries in the south of Europe, so that by 1950 the number of Roman Catholics had grown to about 28,000,000. But the 51,000,000 Protestants represent the growth of the churches that have been longest in this country, and with the decrease in immigration the comparative growth in the number of Roman Catholics is likely to fall off.

But there is another question that will be asked. Are the people better, and is the life of the country better, for what the churches have stood for all through the 1800's and the 1900's, and stand for now?

Of course the answer to *that* question cannot be put into figures of arithmetic. No one can exactly say that on account of Christianity some person or some town that was half good last year is two-thirds good this year. The change that comes through the churches cannot be measured with a yardstick or weighed on a scale. But it can be seen and felt, like a change in the weather from a gray day to a sunny one that makes the world seem a better place in which to be alive. It would be hard to find anyone who would say he wished that the country in which we and our fore-fathers grew up had been a country with no churches in it—no sound of church bells on Sunday mornings, no coming together of friends and neighbors to think again of God, no prayers and no thanksgiving, no reminder from the Bible of God's grace that can forgive sins and strengthen all who want to be braver and truer. A great man wrote once to a boy who was going away from home, "Nail the flag of your convictions to the masthead, and keep it there. Many a person, looking back over part of his life, has wished that he had been a better Christian. I have never known anyone who wished he had been a worse one."

Christians everywhere would like to think of their particular nation as a "Christian country." Many in the United States would claim that description for their own land. As a matter of fact there is no country that comes near to being fully Christian. So far as their actual interests and behavior go, multitudes of people could better be called pagan. But every country in which the Church has been alive and active has in it a leaven that will go on working always. It knows the Ten Commandments. It has heard the Sermon on the Mount and all the other teaching of Jesus. And in its thought and possible ideals it can never get away from all that it has learned of what the apostle Paul called the "mind of Christ."

CHAPTER 33

WHAT THE CHURCHES
MAY BE LEARNING NOW

N THE United States, as in other countries, the Roman Catholic Church is part of a great organization that has the center of its rule in Rome. All its life and thought assume the pope's authority. In 1870 it was proclaimed that when the pope speaks ex cathedra, which means from his throne as head of the Church, he can make no error. When the pope declares that such and such is Christian truth, then bishops, priests, and all Roman Catholic people must accept it. And the pope himself is bound by the tradition that the popes before him cannot have erred. It is held that what is to be considered as the mind of Christ must be in line with what the Roman Church has declared already.

But the churches that are the heirs of Protestant thought are freer to try to discover what the mind of Christ may be for new times and new conditions. Here then are some of the ways in which the churches not bound to Rome may be learning more largely the mind and purpose of the living Lord:

First, as the spirit of truth.

One of the great things that the Reformation did was to make men face searching questions and try to find honest answers. They began to realize that some of what they had been taught to think might not be so. Could their teachers have been mistaken? Was it possible that the Church itself might have been mistaken? To speak out such an idea as that seemed shocking and outrageous to those who thought that no fixed authority should be disturbed. But the reformers dared to believe that the Church ought to be disturbed and even shaken to its foundations if that was necessary to shatter old walls that had shut out truth and to build something greater in their place.

And that was what happened again, though in a new and different way, in the middle of the 1800's. There began to be astonishing new discoveries about the earth and about life upon it. A study of the rocks and of the bones of creatures embedded in them that must have lived ages and ages ago when the layers of the earth were formed showed that everything must be vastly older than the opening pages of the Bible had been supposed to say. And other discoveries of the scientists and the historians broke up the comfortable opinions in which many Church teachers had felt at home. So there was a frightened outcry. Nobody who was really a Christian could believe the new teachings that seemed so contrary to what everybody had considered to be the ways of God!

This was what many people were declaring. But the braver ones in the churches were like the brave men of the Reformation. They believed that every new truth men dared to follow would make them not less sure but more sure of the greatness of God. They were ready to have their knowledge of everything, including the Bible, examined and enlarged. Religion must have adventure in it. That is what the churches in the last century have been discovering. In a larger way than had been understood before, John Robinson was right when he told the pilgrims as they set sail from Holland that "there is always more truth ready to break forth out of God's holy Word."

The spirit of truth has moved in the churches also in education. Far back in the earliest years of the colony of Massachusetts it was the religious devotion of the colonists that in 1636 made them establish Harvard College. This is the way they described what they were doing and why they did it:

After God had carried us safe to *New England,* and wee had builded our houses, provided necessaries for our liveli-hood, rear'd convenient places for God's worship, and settled the Civil Government: One of the next things we longed for, and looked after was to advance *Learning* and perpetuate it to Posterity, dreading to leave an illiterate ministry to the Churches, when our present Ministers shall lie in the Dust.

Harvard did not stand alone. Even before Harvard was

founded, a school for the Indians had been planned in Virginia. Its actual establishment was prevented because part of the settlement was overrun and many of the settlers killed by a sudden Indian attack. But before the end of the century men of the Church of England had founded the college of William and Mary. Soon afterward the Congregationalists established Yale College in Connecticut, and in New Jersey the Presbyterians started Princeton. Besides these and other colleges that sprang up along the Atlantic coast, new ones were planted, especially by the Methodists, the Lutherans, and the Baptists, as the settlers pushed the frontiers farther to the west. Nobody is surprised now to see schools and colleges everywhere. But there was a time when none of them existed, and it was because of the churches that the first of them began.

If the churches thus have valued knowledge and tried to be loyal to truth, that is good. But that is not enough. Something more has always been needed if it was to seem that the churches had the "mind of Christ."

The prophet Micah once asked a question that had its own answer in it. "What doth the Lord require of thee," he asked, "but to do justly, and to love mercy, and to walk humbly with thy God?"

Take part of that saying first—"to do justly and to love mercy." Anyone who remembers the life of Jesus and reads his Sermon on the Mount will understand that no one can genuinely be a Christian unless he wants to be just and merciful.

But being just and merciful is not as easy or as simple as it might sound. Actually it may be easier for people to find what they think are quite natural reasons for not being either. And in the United States in the 1800's there were things that only men of fine conscience saw to be unjust and cruel. There was the fact of slavery. Black men and women from the tribes in Africa were caught by white men, herded on ships, and brought to English colonies and to America to be sold and put to work.

Something else was growing up that was not called slavery but was not much different. This was the kind of work that went on in mills and factories. For the first time since the world began men had discovered how to harness steam and turn it into power. Then machines were developed to be run by steam, and factories were built to hold the machines and thousands of men and women and children brought in to keep the machines going. They had lived before in the little villages or in the open country. Now they worked in the factories all day for wages hardly enough to keep them alive, and went back at night to nasty hovels in the streets and alleys of the crowded towns. But many people who were making money looked at all this without any shame or pity. This was the way things had to be, they said, if there was to be prosperity. The men with most brains had a right to get rich. If poor people got the worst of it, that was their own concern; and they would just have to make out the best way they could.

At the same time there were other cruelties that people wrapped up in their own affairs did not care about. Insane people—and many who would not have been insane if they had been kindly treated—were shut up in asylums that were like pens for animals. Nobody except their own families—and they might be too poor to do anything—bothered about the blind or crippled. As for those who got in trouble with the law, they were locked up in filthy jails and prisons with punishments so brutal that they were worse than the crimes that had put the prisoners into jail.

It would be a long way from the truth to say that every church, or the whole of any church, was stirred in conscience by evils such as these. A church, like the ark, may seem to have different sorts of creatures in it. But the Church, like the ark, is meant to start something better on the earth. People in the churches, like people outside them, are born with the same old human nature that makes them think mostly of themselves. But always in the Church there has been the remembrance of Jesus, which is what makes the Church *be* the Church; and that has stirred the minds of men and women to want to show his spirit. Then they begin to think of others and to help where there is need.

So out of the Church again and again have come leaders filled with God's saving purpose. They have had what one great servant of God called a "passion of pity for the poor." They have been indignant when they saw injustice; and wherever there has been suffering, they have had mercy.

In England in the early 1800's William Wilberforce in Parliament began to stir the conscience of England against the slave trade. The Earl of Shaftesbury made people see the evils that were going on in mills and factories, and down in the mines where even small children were being harnessed to drag the coal carts. John Howard devoted his life to stopping the stupid cruelties that went on in jails and prisons. And that same spirit spread to America.

So at length slavery was done away with. Protection and more justice have been given to the people who work. Decent treatment for those accused of crime has gradually developed in place of the old barbarities. Hospitals beyond counting have been built for the sick and schools for the blind and deaf and crippled. People have learned to be sorry for suffering wherever it may be, and immense sums of money have been sent from America to victims of plagues or floods or earthquakes in far countries of the earth. Slowly also there has grown up a new feeling of the wickedness of war and an effort to bring the nations together to prevent it. Help for those to whom sudden disaster may come is not left to chance but provided for by the Red Cross. And through its very name everyone can see that back of the Red Cross is the spirit of the crucified Christ.

"To do justly, and to love mercy." Then there are those other words to be remembered: "And to walk humbly with thy God."

It is these last words that the churches in America faced as the 1900's moved on past the halfway mark. There was a time when people were tempted to think that perhaps they did not have to concern themselves with God. Everything seemed to be safe and prosperous. The civilization that men had created could be proud of itself. Just by their own abilities men could make life as good as it needed to be.

Then came the two world wars, and proud ideas fell down like a house of cards. So human smartness was not so sufficient after all! Not only is it the frightful destruction that the wars already fought have made. It is the fact that there have been let loose forces that, if the world goes on as it has been going, may destroy it altogether. Men have the power of the atom, but this power that could be a blessing can be instead the whole world's ruin. The question is: Do we have sense enough and self-control enough to be fit to use it? Until men learn another lesson, the answer will be No.

That lesson is what the Church has always proclaimed and what men at last must understand. "Walk humbly with thy God." Our danger is in thinking that if we are smart enough, we can save ourselves. Our need is to know that if we would be saved, we must let God show us our destroying sins. And the deadliest sin could be the pride that makes us think—each one of us or each group of us—that we are all right as we are.

But we are not all right. We may be most wrong in those ways in which we most stubbornly claim that we are right. One nation supposes that it is better than all other nations. One church may suppose it is better than all other churches. But none is good until it humbles itself before the goodness of God and tries to be teachable by his will.

And our hope is that we may be learning. What the apostle Paul wrote long ago is forever true: that "none of us liveth to himself, and none dieth to himself." Because men see that, they are trying to build the United Nations. Because the churches see it, they are trying to draw closer together.

As against the unity and strength of the Church of Rome the weakness of the churches that accepted the free spirit of the Reformation is their division. Besides the churches that have been mentioned, there are many others. In any country where liberty of belief and conscience are allowed, there are bound to be many variations. In the United States among those who want to be counted as Christians are groups as far off on opposite extremes as the Unitarians, who separated from the Congregationalists of New England because the orthodox theology about Christ and the Calvinistic doctrines seemed to them unreal; and the Latter Day Saints, or Mormons, who follow their prophet Joseph Smith, who said that an angel had appeared to him and showed him where to find a golden book of revelation; and the Seventh-day Adventists, who look for a second coming of Christ that may happen any day.

For a long time the divisions among those who might belong to the Christian family were accepted as something that had to be. But now there is a change. In 1908 most of the greater Protestant denominations in the United States and some of the smaller ones formed the Federal Council of the Churches of Christ, to understand one another better and to plan and work together in as many ways as they could. And in 1950 this was enlarged and strengthened as the National Council. Moreover, some churches that had long been separate in the United States, in Canada, and in India have overcome their differences and united.

The desire to end the divisions among Christians is wider than any one country. A National Council is not enough. So at Amsterdam in 1948 representatives from Christian churches in every continent of the earth and from lands as far off as India, China, and Japan met and formed the World Council of Churches. Among these were included not only the branches of the Anglican communion and other churches that have shared the spirit of the Protestant Reformation, but also the Greek Orthodox Church—which has brought to the council its loyal witness to ancient Christian faith and tradition, a richness of worship, and the devotion of its scattered people in spite of many hardships. At Evanston, Illinois, near Chicago, in 1954 the World Council held its second great assembly, with representatives from 163 churches of 48 countries, to think together of "Christ—the Hope of the World."

Still the churches have a long way to go before they reach the desire of Christ that "there shall be one flock, one shepherd." But they are moving toward that hope.

So the long story of the Church has told of what has been. Now it may have its climax in the humble desire for what may come to be. Christians everywhere can lift up to God their prayer for the Church, that he may

fill it with all truth, in all peace. Where it is corrupt, purify it; where it is in error, direct it; where in any thing it is amiss, reform it. Where it is right, establish it; where it is in want, provide for it; where it is divided, reunite it; for the sake of him who died and rose again, and ever liveth to make intercession for us, Jesus Christ, thy Son, our Lord.

INDEX

Accolade, 89
Acts, Book of, 51
Age of Enlightenment, 168
Alaric the Goth, 59 f.
Alban, 46
Albert of Brandenburg, 126, 128
Albigenses, 113 f.
Alcuin, 85
Alexander III, 101
Alexander VI, 121
Ambrose, 56
America, religious settlements in, 158 ff.
Anabaptists, 139, 164
Ananias, 28 f.
Anathema, 99
Andrew, 11
Anne of Bohemia, 117
Anthony, 62
Antioch, 32 f., 92
Apostle, meaning of, 32
Apostles' Creed, 51
Appian Way, 39
Aquinas, Thomas, 113
Arabia, 75
Arius, 52
Armagh monastery, 67
Asbury, Francis, 190
Asia Minor, 33, 36 f.
Athanasius, 52
Athens, 36
Attila the Hun, 60 f.
Augustine of England, 69 ff.
Augustine of Hippo, 57, 59
Augustinian Order, 125
Avignon, 115 ff.

Babylonian Captivity, 115
Baltimore, Lord, 187
Baptism, 53, 80, 139, 146, 165, 190
    of Ambrose, 56 f.
    of Constantine, 49
    of Cornelius, 32
    of Ethelbert, 71
    of Ethiopian officer, 31
    at Pentecost, 22
    of Roger Williams, 163
    of the Saxons, 85
Baptist Church, 163 ff., 177, 187, 189 f.
Barbarians, 59 ff., 66
Barnabas, 30 ff.
Barons, 83 f., 88
Basle, 140

Becket, Thomas, 100 f.
Benedict of Nursia, 63, 65
Benedictine Order, 65
Berea, 36
Bernard of Quintavelle, 105
Bernardone, Pietro, 103 f.
Bible
    authority of, 153
    preaching of, 135, 137 f., 165
    reading of, 145, 160
    as rule of life, 116 f., 129, 138
    translation of, 63, 116, 134, 145, 158,
        179 f.
Bishop of Rome, 61, 74, 95
Bishops, 54, 74, 96 f., 110 f., 161
Black Stone, 75 f.
Bohemia, 117 f.
Boleyn, Anne, 144
Boniface VIII, 115
Boniface (Winfrid), 71 f.
Book of Common Order, 152
Book of Common Prayer, 146 f., 149, 158,
    188
Book of Discipline, 152
Bora, Katherine von, 135
Bradford, William, 160
Britain, invasion of, 66
Bunyan, John, 164 f.
Burma, missions in, 180
Byzantine Empire, 73
Byzantium, 73

Caiaphas, 15, 24
Calvary, 16
Calvin, John, 140 ff.
Cambridge University, 88, 145
Campbell, Alexander, 190
Campbell, Thomas, 190
Canterbury Cathedral, 71
"Canticle of the Sun," 108
Carey, William, 177 ff.
Cardinals, 115
Catacombs, 43
Cathanii, Peter, 105
Cathedrals, 110 ff.
Catherine of Aragon, 143 f., 146 f.
Catholic Church, 74 f., 139. *See also*
    Church of Rome
Catholic, meaning of, 75
Centurion at Calvary, 16
Charlemagne, 85 f., 96
Charles I, 163 f., 168

Charles II, 164, 166 f.
Charles V, 130 f., 134, 143
Chastity, vow of, 154 f.
Children's Crusade, 92 f.
China, missions in, 180
Chivalry, age of, 88 f.
Christ. *See* Jesus Christ
Christians
  behavior of, 40 f., 54
  beliefs of, 51 ff., 74, 81, 121 f., 161
  courage of, 44 ff., 117 f., 166
  name of, 33
  persecution of, 24 ff., 41 ff., 62, 114 f., 121,
    139, 147, 151, 176
  pledge of loyalty of, 51
Chrysostom, John, 74, 79
Church
  authority of, 61, 81 f., 95 ff., 116
  beginnings of, 11
  buildings of, 110 f.
  corruption in, 115 ff., 120 f., 140, 187
  councils of, 56, 74, 153
  criticism of, 113 ff., 120 f., 129, 140, 161,
    168 f.
  divisions of, 74 f., 96, 153, 187
  fellowship of, 189
  growth of, 22 f., 49, 50, 192
  indifference of, 169
  influence of, 193
  law of, 74, 142, 164
  membership of, 192
  ministry of, 53 f., 146, 169
  power of, 81 f.
  prosperity of, 55
  purifying of, 97, 138, 187
  social achievements of, 198 f.
  unity of, 201
Church of England, 46, 149, 158, 161, 163,
  166 ff., 176, 187 f.
Church of Rome, 74 f., 122, 153 ff., 200. *See
  also* Popes
Church of Rome, authority of, 61, 95,
  100 f., 115, 153
Circus Maximus, 41
City of God, The, 59, 85
Clement VII, 143 f.
College of William and Mary, 196
Columba, 68 f.
Communion, 13 f., 41, 53, 80, 138, 141, 146,
  158, 165
Confessions, 59
Congregationalists, 161, 187
Conscience, freedom of, 163 f., 166, 187
Constantine, 48 f., 52, 54, 60, 73, 95
Constantinople, 60, 73, 92, 120
Constitution of the U. S., 191
Corinth, 36
Cornelius, 32
Council of Clermont, 91 f.
Council of Constance, 117 f.

Council of Nicaea, 48 f., 52 f., 56, 74
Council of Trent, 153, 155
Coverdale, Miles, 146
Cranmer, Thomas, 146 ff.
Creed, meaning of, 51
Creeds, 51 ff., 56, 146
Cromwell, Oliver, 163
Cross, sign of the, 48, 53
Crusade, meaning of, 91
Crusades, 91 ff., 100, 113, 119

Damacus, road to, 27 f.
Dante, 120
Dark Ages, 78, 82, 84, 88
"Defender of the Faith," 145
Demetrius, 37
"Deus vult," 91
Devils, belief in, 124
Diana, 37
Diet at Speyer, 134
Diet at Worms, 130 ff., 144
Diocletian, 44, 46, 48
Disciple, meaning of, 32
Disciples
  call of, 11
  courage of, 22, 24
  persecution of, 24 ff.
  resurrection appearances to, 18 f.
Disciples of Christ, 190 f.
Divine Comedy, 120
Dominic, 113 f.
Dominican Order, 113 f.
Drama, medieval, 109 f.
Dutch Reformed Church, 187

Easter, 18
Eck, John, 128
Edict of Milan 48
Education, religious, 195 f. *See also*
  Schools *and* Universities
Edward VI, 146 f., 151
Edwards, Jonathan, 174 f.
Eisleben, 124
Elders, 54, 142
Elijah, 12
Eliot, John, 176
Elizabeth I, 148, 152, 157
Elizabeth II, 149
Emmaus, road to, 18
Emperor worship, 40
England
  church in, 144, 146 ff. *See also* Church
    of England
  evangelism of, 71
  name of, 69
  Reformation in, 143 ff., 155
English Bible, 116, 145 f.
Envy, sin of, 79
Ephesus, 37
Episcopal Church, 188

Erasmus of Rotterdam, 121, 137
Ethelbert, 71
Everyman, 110
Ex cathedra, 194
Excommunication, 98 ff., 117, 121, 134

Faith, justification by, 125
Farel, William, 140 f.
Federal Council of the Churches of Christ, 201
Felix, 37
Feudalism, 83 f.
Florence, 120 f.
Fox, George, 165 f.
France, Reformation in, 139 f., 153
Francis of Assisi, 102 ff.
Franciscan Order, 106, 108, 113
Frederick of Saxony, 130, 133
Friends of God, 122
Frundsberg, 131

Gabriel, 75
Galerius, 46, 48
Geneva, 140 ff., 153
Gentiles, 31 f.
Germany, evangelism of, 71
Gethsemane, 15
Gluttony, sin of, 79
God
    Jesus' teaching about, 12
    judgment of, 80
    revelation in Jesus, 52 f.
    walking humbly with, 199 f.
Godfrey of Bouillon, 92
Gospels, 51
Great Awakening, the, 174
Gregory I, 69
Gregory VII, 97 ff.
Grenfell, Wilfred, 181
Guadalcanal, 185 f.

Hamilton, Patrick, 151
Hampton Court Conference, 158
Harvard University, 195
Hegira, 76 f.
Henry II, 100 f.
Henry III, 96
Henry IV, 98 ff.
Henry VIII, 143 ff.
Heresy, 114, 117, 129
Herod Agrippa, 37 f.
Hilarianus, 43 f.
Hildebrand. *See* Gregory VII
History of Plymouth Plantation, 160 f.
"*Hoc signo vinces*," 48
Holy Land, 77, 91, 100, 119
Holy Roman Empire, 86 f., 96
Holy Spirit, 22, 96, 115, 165, 189
Howard, John, 199
Huguenots, 153, 189

Humanists, 137
Huns, 60 f.
Hunt, Robert, 158
Huss, John, 117 ff., 176, 187
Hymns, writing of, 173

Icons, 96
Idols, 75 f.
Images, 95 f., 138
Imitation of Christ, The, 122
Independents, 160, 163
India, missions in, 179
Indulgences, 126 ff., 135, 137, 146, 153
Infidels, 91
"Inner light," 165
Innocent III, 101, 106, 113 f.
Inquisition, 114 f.
Institutes of the Christian Religion, 140
Interdict, 98
Iona, 68
Ireland, evangelism in, 67 f.
Isadore, 95
Isaiah, 31
Islam, 76

James, 11, 19, 21
James I, 157 f., 163
Jamestown settlement, 158, 161
Jason, 35
Jerome, 63
Jerusalem, 12 f., 77, 92
Jesuits, 153 ff., 158
Jesus Christ
    beliefs about, 52 f., 55 f.
    betrayal of, 13
    as a boy, 20
    charges against, 15, 24
    as the Christ, 12, 25, 28, 35
    cross of, 16
    crucifixion of, 16, 36
    imitation of, 121 f.
    as judge, 81, 124 f.
    mind of, 194, 196
    mocking of, 16
    opposition to, 11 ff.
    Paul's vision of, 28
    persecution of, 28
    praying of, 15
    prediction of death by, 12
    presence of, 53, 138
    remembrance of, 21 f., 31, 81, 198
    resurrection of, 17 ff., 36
    as Savior, 22, 31, 125
    as Son of God, 16, 21
    tomb of, 17 f.
Jews as chosen people, 31
John, 11, 17 f., 21, 24, 51
John Mark, 33 f.
Judas, 13, 19, 22
Judson, Adoniram, 180

Julian the Apostate, 49
Justinian, 73 f.
Justinian Code, 74

Kaaba, 75 f.
Keble, John, 189
Khadija, 75 f.
King
  divine right of, 163
  in feudal society, 84
King James Version, 158
Kingdom of heaven, 13, 15 f., 21, 101
Knighthood, 89 f.
Knox, John, 151 f.
Koran, 76 f.

Lame man, healing of, 24
Last Supper. See Communion
Latimer, Hugh, 147
Latin language, 109, 112, 116, 135
Latter Day Saints, 200 f.
Laud, William, 163
Law, William, 170
Leo I, 60 f.
Leo III, 86
Leo IX, 97
Leo X, 126, 128, 145
Leprosy, 103
Livingstone, David, 181
Lombards, 84
London Missionary Society, 180
Lord's Supper. See Communion
Louis IX, 92
Loyola, Ignatius, 154 f.
Luther, Martin, 124 ff., 144, 187
Lutheran Church, 138, 153, 167

Macedonia, 34
Madras Assembly, 181
Malta, 39
Marriage of clergy, 96 f., 135, 138
Mars Hill, 36
Martel, Charles, 84
Martin, 63
Mary Magdalene, 17 f.
Mary, mother of Jesus, 20 f. See also Virgin Mary
Mary, Queen of Scots, 151 f.
Mary Tudor, 147 f., 151
Maryland, 187 f.
Mass, 80 f., 116, 129, 135, 138, 146, 151
Matthew, 11
Mecca, 75 f.
Medina, 76
Melanchthon, Philipp, 134
Mendaña, 182
Mennonites, 139, 164
Messiah, 12, 33
Methodist Church, 173, 190
Middle (Medieval) Ages, 88 ff., 109 ff.

Milan, 56 f.
Milvian Bridge, Battle of, 48
Missions and missionaries, 66 ff., 176 ff., 187 ff.
Mohammed, 75 ff.
Mohammedans, 76 f.
Monasteries, 62 ff., 71, 78, 110, 124, 135, 154
Monica, 57
Monks, 62 ff., 78, 110, 121, 154
Monte Cassino monastery, 65
Montserrat monastery, 154
Moravian Brethren, 176 f.
More, Thomas, 144
Mormons, 200 f.
Morrison, Robert, 180 f.
Mosque of Omar, 77
Muhlenberg, Henry Melchior, 167
Mystery and morality plays, 109

National Council of the Churches of Christ, 201
Nazareth, 27
Nero, 42
New Amsterdam, 167
New Birth, 119
New Testament, 51, 140, 145. See also Bible
Newman, John Henry, 189
Nicaea, 92
Nicene Creed, 51 ff., 96
Nicholas V, 120
Ninety-five Theses, 127 f.
Noah's Flood, 109
Nobility, 83

Obedience, 142, 154 f.
Orthodox Church, 74, 95 f., 201
Oxford Movement, 189
Oxford University, 88, 116, 145, 189

Packynton, Augustine, 145 f.
Papal court, 121
Passover, 12 f.
Patriarch, 74
Patrick, 66 f.
Patteson, John Coleridge, 183 f.
Paul
  achievements of, 49
  blindness of, 28 f.
  conversion of, 27 ff.
  escape from Damascus of, 29
  execution of, 42
  as great adventurer, 31 ff.
  imprisonment of, 35, 37, 39
  letters of, 51
  name of, 30
  opposes Christians, 25 ff.
  persecution of, 29, 33 ff.
  preaching of, 29 f., 33, 35 f.
  Roman citizenship of, 35

Paul—*cont'd*
  self-defense of, 37 f.
  shipwreck of, 38 f.
  trial of, 38 f.
  vision of, 28, 38
  visits Antioch, 32 f., 36
  visits Asia Minor, 33 f., 36 f.
  visits Athens, 36
  visits Corinth, 36
  visits Ephesus, 37
  visits Jerusalem, 36 f.
  visits Macedonia, 34
  visits Philippi, 35
  visits Thessalonica, 35
Paul III, 155
Pax Romana, 40
Peasants' Revolt, 136
Penn, William, 166 f.
Pennsylvania, 167
Pentecost, 22 ff.
People, common, 11, 83 f., 90, 109, 111, 116,
  121 f., 168
People, rule of the 138
Pepin the Short, 84
Perpetua, 43 f.
Peter
  call of, 11
  denial of, 15, 22
  execution of, 42
  imprisonment of, 24
  letters of, 51
  name of, 21
  preaching of, 22 ff.
  remembers Jesus, 21 f.
  Resurrection and, 17 ff.
  successors of, 61, 74, 95, 153
  vision of, 32
  visits Cornelius, 32
Peter the Hermit, 92
Philadelphia, 167
Philip, 31
Philippi, 35
Pilate, 15 f., 49, 101
Pilgrim's Progress, 165
Plymouth Settlement, 160 ff.
Polycarp, 43
Popes, 74, 85, 95 ff.
  authority of, 95, 120, 144, 151, 153 f.
  choice of, 96
  emperors and, 86 f. 95 ff., 115
  meaning of, 61
Porcius Festus, 37 f.
Poverty, vow of, 105 f., 113 f., 125, 154 f.
Prelates, 116
Presbyterian Church, 142, 152, 163, 189
Presbyters, 54
Pride, sin of, 79
Princeton University, 196
Protestant, 134
Protestant churches, 192 f.

Protestant churches, divisions in, 200 f.
Providence, 163
Provoost, Samuel, 188
Purgatory, 122, 127, 146, 153
Puritans, 158 ff.
Pusey, Edward B., 189

Quakers, 165 f., 187

Ravenna, 73, 84
Red Cross, 199
Reformation, 128 ff., 194
Reformed Church, 138, 153, 167
Religious freedom, 161 ff., 167, 191
Renaissance, 119 f.
Retainers, 89
Revelation, book of, 51
Rhode Island, 162 f.
Richard I, 92
Richard II, 117
Ridley, Nicholas, 147
Robinson, John, 195
Roman Catholic Church, 192, 194. *See also*
  Church of Rome
Roman Empire, 40, 59 f., 73, 83
Rome, 39 ff., 59, 121
Rome, church in, 49. *See also* Church of
  Rome

Sabbath, 23, 158, 160
Sacraments, 53. *See also* Baptism *and* Com-
  munion
St. Bartholomew's Day Massacre, 153
St. Damian's Church, 104
St. Peter's Cathedral, 126
St. Sophia, church of, 60, 73 f.
Saints' relics, 122
Salome, 17
Saul. *See* Paul
Savonarola, 120 f.
Schools, 85, 88. *See also* universities
Schweitzer, Albert, 181
Scotland
  evangelism of, 68 f.
  Reformation in, 149 ff.
Seabury, Samuel, 188
"Seekers," 163
Seleucia, 33
Separatists, 160, 164
Serious Call to a Devout and Holy Life, A,
  170
Seven deadly sins, 79
Seventh-day Adventists, 201
Shaftesbury, Earl of, 199
Silas, 34 f.
Simons, Menno, 139
Sin, forgiveness of, 125, 127
Slavery, 183, 196, 199
Smith, Joseph, 201
Social evils, 197 ff.

Society of Friends, 165
Society of Jesus, 153 ff.
Solomon Islands, 182 f.
Spanish Armada, 149
Spiritual Exercises, 154
Squires, 89
Stephen, 25 28
Stephen III, 84
Summa Theologiae, 113 f.
Sunday, 17, 23, 158, 160
Superstitions, 137
Suttee, 179
Sylvester I, Bishop, 95

Tarsus, 92
Temple of Jerusalem, 13, 16, 23, 77
Tetzel, John, 127 f.
Theodosius, 57
Thessalonica, 35, 57
Thirty Years' War, 168
Thomas, 11
Tournaments, 90
Tours, Battle of, 77, 84
Troas, 34
Truth, spirit of, 194 ff.
Tyndale, William, 145 f.

Unitarian Church, 200
United States, churches in, 187 ff.
Universities, growth of, 88, 113, 195 f. *See also* Schools
University of Erfurt, 124
University of Paris, 88
University of Prague, 117

Upper Room, 20, 53
Urban II, 91, 100

Venice, 119
Vigil of knighthood, 89
Virgin Mary, 81 f., 146
Vulgate, 63

Waldensians, 114 f.
Waldo, Peter, 114 ff.
Wartburg Castle, 134
Wesley, Charles, 170 ff.
Wesley, John, 170 ff., 188, 190
Westminster Confession, 163
White, William, 188
Whitefield, George, 172, 175 f.
Wilberforce, William, 199
Williams, Roger, 162, 187
Winfrid. *See* Boniface
Wishart, George, 151
Witherspoon, John, 189
Wittenberg, 125 ff.
Woodforde, James, 169
World Council of Churches, 201
Worship, freedom of, 48, 160, 174, 187 191
Wotan 71
Wycliffe, John, 116 ff., 144, 187

Xavier, Francis, 155 f.

Yale University, 196

Zinzendorf, Count, 177
Zwingli, Ulrich, 137 ff.